Judaism for Everyone ... without Dogma

"*Judaism for Everyone ... without Dogma represents a major contribution to the advancement of contemporary Judaism. It argues for a secular Judaism rooted in Jewish culture and humanistic and democratic values, for Jewish communities that respect pluralism, for a dialogue between Diaspora and the State of Israel that fosters the richness, and diversity of the Jewish people. For all these reasons, I strongly recommend this book."*
　—Yossi Beilin, Former Israel MP (Member of the Knesset), Minister of Religious Affairs, Justice, Economics and Planning, and leading participant in both the Oslo Accords and the Geneva Peace Initiative.

"*Bernardo Sorj has powerfully articulated the historical, and cultural grounding of the movement of Secular Humanistic Judaism. From the beginnings of Jewish evolution to today's Jewish diversity, his insightful analysis of the modern Jewish experience, and his message of acceptance will resonate with cultural Jews worldwide.*"
　—Rabbi Adam Chalom, Dean, North America, Interna-tional Institute for Secular Humanistic Judaism.

"Judaism for Everyone ... without Dogma *offers a brilliant new approach to the future of an ancient people. Prof. Bernardo Sorj's deep acquaintance with Jewish history, Jewish tradition, and the state of Jews around the world today, led him to the conclusion, that the way to save Judaism from extinction is to take the keys of the*

gates to Judaism from the religious establishment. New Judaism should be pluralistic, democratic, and open to everyone."
  — Nahum Barnea, Political Scientist and Journalist, awarded with the Israel Prize for Communication in 2007.

"Sorj positions humanistic Judaism as an antidote to irrationalism and dogma. He tells how humanistic Jews can embrace the past, without allowing it to dominate the present, by showing how we can simultaneously develop ties to tradition while becoming increasingly open to embracing all of humankind."
  — Roy Speckhardt, Executive Director, American Humanist Association.

"Judaism for Everyone ... without Dogma *provokes deep thinking for Jews and non-Jews alike by exploring the balance between emphasizing universal human aims and preserving the value of unique Jewish cultural history and tradition"*.
  — Yaakov Malkin, Author, and Professor of Aesthetics and Rhetorics at Tel Aviv University (Ret).

"This is a most important book for Jews, and others from varied religious heritages, who wish to transcend narrow denominational viewpoints or have an archaic jaded view of Judaism. It brings Judaism to a level consistent with what we actually believe, and not what we are told to accept. It represents a most articulate, and informative way of thinking of twentieth century western Jewry. I would heartily recommend this work."
  — Al Steiner, Judaic History Scholar

I challenge those who think that "I know all that I need to know" to read Judaism for Everyone ... without Dogma by Prof Bernardo Sorj. It's uniquely written and has the power to change a person's worldview, both Jew and non Jew alike."

—Dr. Edgar Pinto Xavier Th.D., Theologian, Pinto Xavier Institute of Philosophy, Executive Director, Kristang Community for Cultural Judaism, Kuala Lumpur, Malaysia.

"Bernardo Sorj's Judaism for Everyone ... without Dogma provides us with a historical sweep through Jewish history, placing Jews and Judaism in context throughout their development. The book is both stimulating and motivating, allowing a quick yet substantial grasp of a people who have survived, flourished and embraced the times in which they have lived over the centuries. Writing in an accessible style, Sorj posits a Humanistic Judaism which empowers the individual and community rather than stultifying religious or political hegemonies; this augurs well for the future of a culture in transformation."

—Stephen M. Finn, Professor Emeritus, University of Pretoria, South Africa

"......*Secular Culture & Ideas* adheres to a broad definition of Jewish culture, with content driven by an enthusiasm for secular Jewish life. It takes a view of Judaism put forward in the recent publication by Bernardo Sorj, *Judaism for Everyone...without Dogma* where he writes, "Contemporary Judaism is a vast cultural field with porous borders, and that is a good thing. Judaism is a successful synthesis of local and global, particular and universal...[and] is a mixture of destiny and choice...about how to be Jewish. ...Most Jews feel that their Jewish identity should express [these] modern value."

—The Posen Foundation and Myrna Baron, Executive Director of the Center for Cultural Judaism

JUDAISM FOR EVERYONE...
without Dogma

Bernardo Sorj

IFSHJ
www.ifshj.org

Copyright © Bernardo Sorj, 2010
Copyright for the English editions
© The International Federation for Humanist & Secular Judaism and Bernardo Sorj
All rights reserved

ISBN 0-615-35287-1
ISBN13: 978-0-615-35287-9

Adapted from the original Spanish and Portuguese versions by Bernardo Sorj
Translated by Bernardo Sorj, Alexandra Forman and Timothy Thompson

English version edited by Jeanette Friedman, Wordsmithy, LLC

Logo design in text: Iftach Maas; Ikan Maas, ltd

BISAK Identity: REL040000 Judaism/General with sub-categories: 1) Humanistic Judaism, 2) Jews — identity, 3) Judaism — history-philosophy

Library of Congress cataloging-in-Publication Data (a humanistic history and anthology of Judaism's mores, customs and heritage)

Published by the International Federation for Secular & Humanistic Judaism

(0-615-35287-1)
WWW.IFSHJ.ORG

Printed in the United States of America

Contents

Foreword 7
Introduction 9
Part I: A Culture in Transformation 19
 • What Is a Jew? 20
• Biblical Judaism 23
 • The Greco-Roman Period and the Varieties of Judaism 32
• Talmudic Judaism 40
• The Talmudic World of the Middle Ages ... 51
• Jews, Christians, and Muslims 62
 • Modernity: The Return of Philosophy, History, and Politics 67
 • Cultural and Political Movements in Modern Judaism 77

Part II: Contemporary Judaism 90
 • The Holocaust, Memory, and Politics 91
 • The State of Israel: The Challenge of Creating a Secular Democracy 97
 • Postmodernity, Diaspora, and Individualized Judaism 109
 • National Judaisms 115
 • Judaism as Endurance, Cognitive Dissonance, and Collective Guilt 119

Part III: Challenges Facing Judaism 125
 • Who Speaks for the Jews: Rabbis? Plutocrats? The Israeli Government? ... 126
 • Who is Jewish? Weddings and Burials ... 132

- Anti-Semitism and the Relation between *Yidn* and *Goyim*..................................137
- The Future of Judaism..........................144
- The Future of Humanistic and Secular Judaism...147

Appendix: World Jewish Population...........163

Glossary..171

Acknowledgments...176

Suggested Reading...178

Foreword

Discovering the everlasting vibrancy of Judaism demands an effort to absorb the values of the modern world and renew the ways we relate to Judaism's age-old traditions. The book you are about to read is an exciting and contemporary view of Judaism.

We believe that *Judaism for Everyone... without Dogma* can enhance Jewish identity by reintroducing a time-tested Judaism that is an integral part of humankind's never-ending search for self-improvement. The book is authored by Bernardo Sorj, an intellectual, social scientist, and prolific writer whose historical and pluralistic approach to Judaism is supported by his life experiences. He has lived in several countries of the Diaspora and studied Jewish history in Israel. His case is based on realistic humanistic values and not an apologia for an external authority.

Rationality and the search for meaning are the building blocks of this author's discussion of Judaism. His chronological description of Judaism's transfiguration over the ages leads to a modern-day formula that enables us to preserve Jewish heritage and culture. His goal is to present a Judaism that creates mutual respect and understanding between peoples in pursuit of the highest goal of all, peace. The Judaism presented here is a defense against the world's intensifying pandemic of religious bigotry and xenophobia.

Jews have been dispersed into separate enclaves over a vast, hostile world for at least two millennia. They have survived. For centuries, the main unifying influence was Talmudic law. Enlightenment catalyzed developing changes that can lead us to a unifying age of reason and respect for human dignity. Bernardo Sorj has memorialized those changes and leads us to contemporary humanistic thinking while preserving and cultivating the goodness of Judaism.

It is for these reasons that the IFSHJ has published *Judaism for Everyone ... without Dogma*.

It is our hope that, after reading, you too will say, "THIS IS THE JEW I AM."

INTERNATIONAL FEDERATION FOR SECULAR & HUMANISTIC JUDAISM
www.ifshj.org

[signature]

Marvin. A. Rosenblum, President

Efraim Zadoff, V.P.   Yair Lifshitz, V.P.

The umbrella organization of the worldwide Movement for Secular & Humanistic Judaism.

Introduction

This essay is an introduction to a Judaism that I hope will interest Jews and non-Jews alike. It updates the humanistic and secular Judaism that was a hallmark of the greatest modern Jewish thinkers, including Baruch Spinoza, Sigmund Freud, Albert Einstein, Hannah Arendt, Marc Chagall, Franz Kafka, George Gershwin, Arthur Rubinstein, Theodor Herzl, Emma Goldman, and Amos Oz, along with the majority of Nobel laureates.

Each of them in their particular manner advanced modern Judaism as a way of being Jewish without relying on sacred books or divine commandments; instead, they drew on the psychological and existential dramas of Jewish history and culture for their inspiration. They felt a particular sense of solidarity in times of Jewish persecution and revulsion when Jews acted carelessly and caused others to suffer.

This is a necessary update because modern, humanistic Judaism is in crisis. Although the majority of Jews in the Diaspora and in Israel consider themselves to be humanistic, humanistic Judaism has lost much of its original impulse and creativity.

This crisis is a byproduct of the far-reaching transformations that Jewish communities and society in general have undergone in recent decades. We live in a post-socialist and post-Zionist world where Jews feel they are full members of the democratic societies where most of them live.

The different branches of modern Judaism did emphasize its universal ethical dimensions. By doing so, they have concealed the tensions between the diverse identities and loyalties present within each of us. Identification with the suffering and joy of others carries a different weight depending on our various identities—for example, family, religion, gender, ethnicity, nationality. These conflicts exist and will only vanish on the day humanity comes to live in harmony—if that day ever comes.

Until then, the currents of fidelity and solidarity will ebb and flow in each of us, and their relative importance will vary at different times in our lives. There will be times when we feel conflicted about the different parts of our identities, but instead of concealing these tensions we need to make them part of our self-understanding, so that we can better develop our autonomy and sense of personal freedom.

By emphasizing the universal dimensions of Judaism, twentieth-century secular humanistic Judaism came to undermine the justification for the existence of a Jewish identity. If Jewish values are the same as universal values, why maintain a

Jewish identity? Secular humanistic Jews should revalue the particularistic aspects of Jewish tradition and history—without falling into an isolationist attitude based on fear and distrust of the non-Jew, who is sometimes represented in a dehumanizing manner.

The humanistic and progressive vision of history has proved too optimistic. We live in a world charged with political, ethnic, and religious conflict. We cannot avoid acknowledging that Jews around the world can be vulnerable to attack. Otherwise, we might naively facilitate a xenophobic Judaism that feeds on any expression, real or imagined, of anti-Semitism.

Rationality is not the only measure of human history or the only basis of human action. Spirituality—emotions, feelings, and the search for transcendence—are present in every religious and nonreligious human act and are fundamental to social bonds and collective identities. This book does not attempt to avoid the non-rational dimensions of human life; on the contrary, it acknowledges their reality and the challenges they pose to humanistic Judaism.

We should recognize that we are limited in our capacity to shape the world. Such recognition means a humbler view of both our own and each generation's role in history and society. Secular humanistic Judaism has fallen prey to hubris, a feeling of omnipotence that replaces God with humanity and feeds the illusion that the world can be bent to one's will. Such is not the case. Even if God is dead and everything seems possible, we cannot simply substitute man for God and ideology for religion.

On the contrary, we must realize that our ability to understand and shape the world is finite. When religion's answers about the meaning of the universe are no longer satisfying, we must learn to accept the human condition and its unsolvable enigmas. Obviously this self-awareness does not justify moral resignation; in fact, it constitutes a unique source of authentic ethical responsibility based on personal convictions of right and wrong — without expecting God's compensation in this world or an afterlife.

Secular Judaism of the twentieth century was based on "certainties" about the meaning of life and history. Contemporary humanistic Jews value uncertainty as a source of liberty and compassion. Certainties divide and separate, while uncertainty, doubt and fear in face of the unknown, suffering and death, put the human condition in its proper dimension.

Institutionalized religion recognizes that doubt invades even the most fervent believer — and represents a moment of weakness that needs to be fought. That is why "blind" faith is demanded of believers. Secular people from the most diverse cultural traditions live with doubt and uncertainty in all aspects of their lives. But for them doubt is experienced as something that enhances our humanity, motivates our curiosity, allows us to value other cultures, and leaves us open to new responses.

In all areas of life, the right to doubt is a fundamental value, and the stifling of doubt leads to oppression in all its manifestations. When we exercise our right to doubt, we become empowered as free persons. Notwithstanding, we still need collective beliefs if we are to build community and advance collective action. Our challenge, then, is to foster communities that recognize the value of doubt and nurture individuals who will use their doubt to enrich their communities.

The hubris of twentieth-century secularists in relation to human history and society also applies to Judaism. Hubris led many secularists to scorn aspects of Jewish cultural traditions, which for centuries had been expressed through religious narratives. The secular Zionists, in addition, denied the richness and diversity of Jewish cultural life in the Diaspora and its role in the survival of Judaism.

While we may disagree with and criticize other streams of Judaism, we cannot ignore the contributions of each one, even when we find many aspects of their practice unacceptable to us. In the end, we should be pluralists, not as an expression of mere tolerance for difference, but in recognizing the limitations of every worldview and the richness of diversity.

When a Jew defines him or herself as an agnostic or atheist, he or she is following a general trend in modern thought that questions the existence of God.

But he or she is also echoing a particular doubt about the capacity of the Jewish God to provide convincing answers about the meaning of life in general and Judaism in particular.

Secular movements within Judaism were initially constructed in response to religious tradition, which was experienced as an oppressive and paralyzing force. Without a doubt, this was a correct diagnosis at the time. It is not by chance that those who developed Yiddish culture and the Modern Hebrew language, founded the State of Israel or who fought in the Warsaw Ghetto Uprising were mostly secular Jews. On the other hand, the twentieth century has taught us that atheism can also be an inquisitorial and totalitarian ideology. In the name of atheism, totalitarian regimes have tried to impose their beliefs on others, just as religious leaders try to impose beliefs and values in the name of God.

Today, new religious movements are embracing humanistic values and open dialogue — in opposition to dogmatism, authoritarianism, and the revival of fundamentalism. These new movements have emerged from open societies where individuals and groups can advance their own view of the world without fearing external sanctions.

Therefore the main dividing line for Judaism today is not whether God exists, which is a personal issue. The real division is between those who accept a pluralistic view of Judaism, encompassing all Jews, and those who want to establish a monopoly on their own distinct form of Judaism; between those who believe men and women to have equal rights and those who believe women have fewer rights; between those who condemn homosexuality and those who believe that sexuality and other mores are matters of personal choice; between those who use religion to impose their "truths" in the public sphere and those who believe in democracy, dialogue, and separating worldly politics from transcendental belief.

What distinguishes a humanistic Jew is not belief in God, keeping kosher or using a kippah. The humanistic Jew (regardless of belief in God) respects the human dignity of all people and does not allow a collective identity to be used to dehumanize those who hold different beliefs. Humanistic Judaism is an effort to constantly renew tradition so that its values dignify every human being.

For all of these reasons, humanistic Judaism is deeply linked to the defense of democracy. Freedom of thought, respect for the dignity of every human being, and social justice are its fundamental values. They are to be anchored in institutions that ensure the practice of these rights and the achievement of new ones. Democracy is fundamental to the State of Israel and is the only safeguard for a life of peace and dignity for Jews in the Diaspora. Democracy should also be the standard of every Jewish community's internal life. Unity and diversity coexist through dialogue, respect, and the ability to live within the tensions naturally generated by Judaism's diverse branches.

In recent decades, changes within Judaism have accelerated, causing insecurity within many Jewish institutions that often suppress or distance dissonant voices. Albert Hirschman argues in his book, *Exit, Voice, and Loyalty*, that when the organizations we belong to do not work properly, our first reaction is to express our dissatisfaction, to use our voices.

But our inclination toward protest depends on our degree of loyalty and our will not to jump ship. If our voices are not heard, our loyalty decreases, and many individuals may opt to leave Judaism altogether. Although their decision should be respected, in the end it is impoverishing—because it implies removal from an enriching tradition—and if we can prove our case, this abandonment of Judaism becomes unnecessary.

The winds of change are blowing within Judaism, and the vast majority of Jews are increasingly drawn toward new forms of thought and practice, unburdened by the fear of innovation or anxiety about breaking with the old religious or secular models. Judaism today is extremely diverse and rich, although many Jews are unaware of these new ways to celebrate being Jewish.

This new Judaism is based not on fear of persecution but on pride in being part of an extremely creative culture and history. It is enriched by the interchange between *yidn* (Jews) and *goyim* (non-Jews), and it does not resort to self-exclusion or isolation.

Like all cultural identities, Judaism is a mixture of destiny and choice. For almost two thousand years, historical circumstance has made being Jewish a matter of fate. Now it is becoming more and more a matter of individual choice: a choice to be Jewish and a choice about how to be Jewish; to be born into Judaism and to want to continue to be Jewish; to be Jewish and to want one's children to be Jewish also; not to be born Jewish and to decide to share one's life with Jews and raise Jewish children; or simply deciding to identify with Jewish culture and its collective life.

Judaism has survived by reinventing itself and adapting to new circumstances. I hope this book contributes to identifying new trends within Judaism and to promoting a pluralist vision of Judaism. Answers to questions like Who are we? What path should we follow? will always convey tensions and contradictions.

Individualism and solidarity often collide, as do the values of particularism and universalism. Living freely means making choices, which makes us responsible for reconciling different values in an ongoing effort to seek out and provide creative answers. And for Judaism, freedom means that the issue at stake is not what it is to be a Jew — it means learning how to choose and advance the type of Jew one wants to be.

PART ONE

A CULTURE IN TRANSFORMATION

What Is a Jew?

To define someone or something, we use classificatory systems and concepts that allow us to identify an entity as part of a group of similar phenomena and to differentiate it from the rest. From experience we know that all classificatory systems are limited. No one likes to be "boxed in," for each individual reality is multifaceted and in constant transformation. We also know that general systems of classification, as much as they are necessary, are too narrow to account for complex cultural phenomena. Furthermore, the concepts that we normally use are based on the dominant culture, thus hindering our ability to comprehend other ways of experiencing and interpreting social life.

We generally characterize Judaism as a religion, culture, ethnicity, or collective identity. Why such a variety of definitions? Because each of these definitions emphasizes a specific dimension of Judaism. No single definition is sufficient to capture the richness of the Jewish condition, whose reality resembles more the image of an onion, formed of diverse layers, than of a fruit with a central core.

Consider this: Jewish Orthodox law does not reject the Jewishness of a person who has been born to a Jewish mother or has converted in accordance with his or her particular rules—even if that person comes to define him or herself as an atheist, becomes anti-religious, or converts to another religion. In turn, the great majority of Jews who do not consider themselves religious still participate, to a greater or lesser degree, in rites and ceremonies that have a Jewish religious origin or religious content. The State of Israel defines a person who has a Jewish grandparent as Jewish, entitled to receive citizenship. In practice, Judaism has an inherently pluralistic identity and, being many things at the same time, does not fit within rigid and unequivocal systems of classification.

As a result, some scholars propose more general ways to classify Judaism—like Jewish civilization, Jewish culture, tribe, and/or family. These categories can be useful, and the broader they are, the better. But we must not forget that each time we search for a dimension that defines Judaism, what we are emphasizing is the one specific aspect of it that we happen to value most.

Despite the definition given it by each group or individual, Judaism is a reality that is under constant (re)construction. Made up of many changing emotions and feelings, it contains the diversity of each individual's experience, which includes the experience of one's parents and grandparents—and by extension the culture and psychology of an entity that has three thousand years of history behind it. The ways in which these elements permeate the identity of each Jew are varied and personal, and they change throughout the course of one's life.

Judaism is fragmented, and all of its fragments are equally important. It is not and cannot be homogeneous, and no one branch should deride the others, even though what others believe or practice may offend someone else's sensibilities.

The fragmentation of Judaism is precisely what generates the richness and vitality of 13 million Jewish people in the modern world. We should not attempt to avoid tension and the clash of ideas, for they are fundamental to our self-awareness. One may even proselytize—why not?—in favor of his or her position as long as he or she does not take from another the legitimate right to express his or her Judaism differently.

Although this book does not pretend to present a synthesis of Jewish history, to understand where we find ourselves today we must refer, even if only summarily, to the diverse historical periods that crystallized various models of Judaism. These models are the basic norms—the sensibilities, practices, and discourses—that connect individuals to Judaism. This examination of the past will show that what we assume are natural forms of Judaism are the products of decisions made under specific historical circumstances.

Therefore, they can be changed.

Biblical Judaism

Whether or not one believes that the Bible is the word of God, and whether or not one believes that what is written within it is true, the Bible remains the key text for Jews because it contains the founding myths that shape their collective memory. The Bible presents archetypes and narratives of a common origin that live in the imagination of both Jews and non-Jews: Abraham's founding role, Moses' leading of the Exodus out of Egypt, and David's consolidation of the Kingdom of Israel, from which three thousand years of history would unfold.

This is one possible interpretation of the Bible. Its significance has been redefined by other religions, and it has been analyzed as a literary or historical text. That Christianity and Islam, the other two great monotheistic religions, have attributed different meanings to the Bible is a constitutive part of the cultural context within which Jewish culture developed and continues to be shaped today.

The Bible or *TaNaCh* (Torah [Pentateuch], *Nevi'im* [Prophets], and *Ketuvim* [Writings]) is a compilation of 24 books (some count them as 22) that interlaces individual and collective stories with legislation and collective belief. The Bible narrates the emergence of the people of Israel and contains diverse images of God and his relation to the Jews. God is given many names, possibly referring to deities from the various tribes, including *Elohim*, which means "gods" in the plural. In the Torah, the God of the Jews enters into conflict with other local gods, and the cult of the goddess Asherah is mentioned along with sacrifices "for Azazel."

The Bible juxtaposes various oral traditions from different eras, elaborated over the course of nearly a millennium; it is a complex text that contains diverse influences and differing and repetitive versions of commandments and events. Rather than a single coherent product, we have a text that does not constitute a philosophical treatise or a guide to ethical principles. It tells the story of a community in the process of making its own history. It portrays that community in all its contradictions, fragility, and grandiosity, and it contains multiple heroes and commandments that permit the most varied of readings.

In this complexity we find both the strength and weakness of the Bible. Its diverse stories are subject to different meanings and are the substrata on which later generations constructed their own interpretations in order to resolve the tensions and contradictions of the original text. In large part, the history of Judaism is that of the relationship among the original biblical text, its constant (re)interpretation, and the various uses to which it has been put.

The canonical version of the Bible emerged during Persian rule, possibly in the fourth or fifth century BCE. The Persian emperors of the time were followers of Zoroastrianism, a proto-monotheistic religion that influenced Judaism and predisposed the Emperors Cyrus II and Darius I toward a sympathetic view of Judaism.

The Bible is not chronological and orderly. The biblical text reflects diverse authors who express different beliefs and interests, including those of the priests, the monarchy, and their critics. It resembles a movie compiled of many different moments pieced together and edited haphazardly. For example, the Ten Commandments are mentioned in the period of the Exodus from Egypt—but they were actually codified much later. Philological studies, which identify the relative antiquity of the language in different biblical texts, explain how Israel evolved in its ways of representing God—going from polytheism to national monotheism (which did not exclude the existence of other gods) to exclusive monotheism. These studies also reveal shifting representations of God's alliance with the Israelites and the Jews' place in the world.

The first collection of books, the Torah (comprising Genesis, Exodus, Leviticus, Numbers, and Deuteronomy), opens with God's creation of the world, living beings, and the first man and woman (offering two separate versions of this last event). The genesis of humanity's history is told in short episodes related to the sons of Adam, the construction of the Tower of Babel, and the Flood. After the Flood (which only Noah's family and the animals he had taken aboard the ark survived), God made an alliance with humanity wherein he promised never again to destroy all living beings, as long as they pledged obedience to the so-called seven Noachide Laws, which include the prohibition of murder.

The rest of the Torah tells of the developments and setbacks in the relationship between God and the Jews, beginning with Abraham's departure from his parents' home for a distant land and his readiness to sacrifice his son Isaac in accordance with God's instruction. In the end, God orders him to sacrifice a ram and circumcise Isaac instead — a ritual that becomes the symbol of God's covenant with Abraham and his descendants. If Abraham and his descendants will obey God's commandments, God promises them the land of Canaan and numerous progeny.

Following the story of Abraham is the saga of his son Isaac and grandson Jacob, who after fighting with God (or an angel sent by God) receives the name Israel ("one who has prevailed with God") and whose sons originate the twelve tribes of Israel. The sons of Jacob's son Joseph beget the tribes of Ephraim and Menashe, but Jacob's daughter Dinah does not produce a tribe because the line of descent is patrilineal. Famine in Israel leads Jacob and his sons to Egypt, where they are later enslaved, initiating a new stage in Jewish history.

Under Moses' leadership, the Israelites (and other nations, according to the Bible) are led out of Egypt. The people of Israel then receive the laws that will be the new basis of their alliance with God. They promise to obey the "divine commandments," and God, for his part, will protect them if they obey — or punish them if they do not.

The commandments associated with Moses also detail the sacrifices that should be offered to God to ensure the livelihood of the priests. The laws describe what is pure and impure, particularly in relation to dietary laws and sexual relations, dress codes, and contact with certain types of illness, menstruating woman, and the dead. Laws that separate social acts and relations into pure and impure acts exist in every culture. The laws also include injunctions such as letting the land lie fallow every seven years. Laws that relate to sex, incest, and not wasting sperm (the prohibition of masturbation, homosexuality, and bestiality) are possibly connected to the wish for population growth. All of these responses are designed to differentiate Israel's religion from the practices accepted by the neighbors' cultures, which included child sacrifice.

The biblical text makes an effort to distance Judaism from the fertility rites and nature cults of neighboring tribes, although it never completely succeeds. The biblical festivities continue to reflect a strong relationship with the cyclical rhythms of an agricultural economy.

The Torah establishes what is probably the most original Jewish contribution to human civilization — *Shabbat* (the Sabbath), the weekly day of rest. Other commandments seek to ensure a system of impartial judgment, a periodic liberation of slaves, love for the stranger, laws about loans, and forms of harvesting that leave gleanings for the poor.

In the Book of Prophets, the narrative continues to follow the vicissitudes of the occupation of Canaan, the fights among local tribes led by judges—ad hoc leaders—and the emergence of the monarchy, an institution God had advised against. The monarchy faces dynastic conflicts that divide the tribes of Israel into two separate entities: Judea, whose capital was Jerusalem, and Israel, whose capital was Samaria. Finally, we read of the destruction of both the kingdom of Samaria and its Temple by the Assyrians (722 BCE) and the kingdom of Judea and the Temple of Jerusalem by the Babylonians (586 BCE). The historical narrative ends with the events associated with the reconstruction of the Second Temple of Jerusalem, made possible by the return of the exiled elite under the authorization of the Persian emperor Cyrus.

The prophets occupy a central place in Judea and Samaria and during the Babylonian exile. They admonish the kings and the people for disobeying the divine commandments; they explain the past and foretell the future. The Bible constructs a story about a numerically small people who manage to confront their more powerful enemies thanks to their alliance with God. What could have happened to this alliance? The great challenge of the prophets is to explain the destruction and exile of the kingdoms of Israel and Judea. The prophets argue that when the kings and people disobey the commandments, God removes his protection from Israel.

The great emperors serve as divine instruments to punish the Jewish people, but the pact between Israel and God continues inviolate. Finally, with the coming of the Messiah, Israel will recuperate its splendor and become *ohr lagoyim* ("a light unto the nations").

The Messiah, in the biblical tradition, is an individual with a special mission, a person anointed with olive oil as a sign of divine election, just like the priests, judges, and kings. The Book of Prophets gives the coming of the Messiah new meaning: The Messiah is presented as a leader of the people and as the creator of a new era of peace and prosperity. In this way, the prophets invented the first version of universal history as told from the point of view of a small, defeated nation:Tthe rise and fall of emperors became an instrument of God's will.

The prophetic narrative marks the transition from national monotheism to universal monotheism and consolidates the idea of a chosen people distinct from all others. This status will be confirmed again on the day the Messiah comes. Messianic hope introduced a new dimension into Judaism, allowing Jews to surmount their present-day suffering through the expectation of future redemption. In some texts, messianic redemption is prophesied not only for Jews, but for the rest of humanity as well.

The prophets' vision transformed the Jewish perception of the meaning of history and the role of Jews within it. Instead of explaining historical events as the result of divine will, destiny, or chance, the prophets linked the fate of the Jewish people to their conduct. This produced both the internalization of moral responsibility and a sense of individual and collective guilt, which in turn generated disproportionate suffering because of the assumption that whatever happens to individuals and groups is a consequence of their actions.

The Bible offers an enormous variety of individual and collective dramas that permit diverse interpretations and may lend inspiration to a wide range of beliefs and values. It contains examples of fights for liberation from oppression (such as the Exodus from Egypt), laws of social justice, and ethical principles (such as "Thou shalt love thy neighbor because he is like you"). However, it also contains commandments far removed from contemporary humanistic values: in particular, the imposition of severe punishment on those who disobey the commandments themselves.

The strength of the Bible lies also in its ambiguities. It emphasizes conflict, human fragility, and the human characteristics of God. Yet many modern readers have difficulty accepting a text in which God appears to possess not only compassion and justice but also rage and destruction. Stories like the ones describing the ten plagues suffered by the Egyptians or the total destruction of the people of Jericho or the Korach family (who opposed God's decision to appoint his brother's family to the priestly caste) are hardly edifying. The Torah possesses moral principles and tales of social justice that continue to be valid and others that, if taken literally by fundamentalist readers, would support unacceptable acts of violence, intolerance, and cruelty.

In fact, the Bible contains multiple models of Judaism. It reveals the political and social conflicts between those who wanted to appoint a king and those who opposed monarchic rule. Ruth is listed in King David's genealogy even though she is a Moabite, from one of the tribes cursed by the Torah. The Song of Songs, an extremely sensual text, and Ecclesiastes, a pessimistic text in which God is practically absent, demonstrate the versatility of the Bible. And prophetic discourse often reaches horizons of universality extending far beyond the land of Israel.

Biblical leaders are portrayed as human beings marked by both greatness and shadow: Abraham is a negotiator but also fanatical to the point of sacrificing his own son; Moses is a statesman and legislator who doubts his ability to lead his people; Samson is a hero who defends the Israelites with his own life but feels attracted to the pagan world with its orgies and women; David is the diminutive warrior who confronts the giant Goliath and transforms Jerusalem into the capital but who is, at the same time, attracted to the wife of his general, a man he sends to his death on the battlefield; Solomon is a sage but also an idolater preoccupied with the expansion of his kingdom.

In the Bible, we find the central themes and values that become the prism through which Jews will interpret their historical experience: the promised land, the alliance with God, Jerusalem, the Diaspora, enemies who seek to destroy the people of Israel, internal divisions, dependence on the geopolitical context, conflicts between political and religious interests, tensions between the form and content of the commandments, and the expected arrival of the Messiah. But above all—and this stands as the Bible's most profound mark on the collective psyche of the Jews—we find the history of a tiny population located at the crossroads between Asia and Africa in the heart of the ancient world. This small group of people, destined to be destroyed by the passage of empires, nevertheless did overcome all its setbacks and find the strength to survive.

The obstinate will to continue existing against all odds led the prophets to believe that empires were Jehovah's instrument and that God would redeem his people through the coming of the Messiah. This capacity to resist, this resilience, made possible the existence of the Bible itself, a document about a people who survived multiple defeats and managed to tell its story, a story that until then had been written and interpreted by the powerful and victorious.

The Greco-Roman Period and the Varieties of Judaism

From early on, the small, dry territory of Israel had pushed part of its population into emigration. After the destruction of the First Temple, the elite went into exile in Babylon, a city that became a major center of Jewish cultural life for a millennium. A large number of Jews were already living outside the land of Israel before the destruction of the Second Temple (70 CE), although its population was only radically reduced after the Bar Kokhba uprising against the Roman emperor Hadrian (132–135 CE). The importance of the Diaspora is indicated by Flavius Josephus, a first-century Judeo-Roman historian who writes that those who rose in Israel against the Roman Empire had expected Jews in the Diaspora to send weapons and support.

In his book *Moses*, Martin Buber notes that a central characteristic of the Jews is that they are a wandering people who absorb elements from surrounding cultures. External influences modify Jewish culture, which in turn transforms the original meaning of those influences through a process of assimilation. Buber describes how practically all the elements in the Bible, beginning with language and writing, were taken from other Middle Eastern cultures by the Hebrews. History shows that many practices and ideas from surrounding societies were indeed adapted, including the rejection of polygamy for monogamy in the time of Rabbenu Gershon (960–1028 CE), a Jewish scholar and interpreter of the law who was influenced by Catholic practice.

The elites responsible for elaborating and codifying the "official" position considered external influences to be a problem that demanded an intellectual redefinition of the canon. Foreign influences are more dramatically experienced in open cultural contexts, as in modern times, or as they were during the Greco-Roman period. In times of external aggression it is easier to close off and defend the inherited culture from foreign incursion. But in open cultural exchanges when foreign influences are subtly imposed through example and argument, tradition goes into crisis. Elites become divided over how to integrate the new ways into the inherited cultural world.

Comparison between historical periods has its obvious limitations, since history never repeats itself, but important similarities can be drawn between the Greco-Roman period and modern times. The first experiment in cultural "globalization" was initiated by Alexander the Great (356–323 BCE) and completed during the centuries of the Pax Romana. It ended when the Roman imperial power transformed Christianity into the state religion in the third century CE.

Under the aegis of Hellenism, which extended across the Mediterranean and Middle East, the most diverse cultural traditions coexisted, interacting with and influencing each other. The result was the emergence of new versions of old cultures and religions, including Judaism and the religions that sprang from it—Christianity and, later on, Islam.

Greco-Roman culture, in which the polis was the epicenter of life, was buoyed by Greek philosophy and polytheism and remained open to an array of religions and beliefs. In that world, one would find the lyceum, theater, circus, gymnasium, and baths— all of which radiated cultural values and a particular lifestyle. These influences penetrated Judaism and divided it into different religious currents, political parties, and social movements, all of which faced off within the same tradition.

In the Hellenistic world, each current within Judaism integrated new beliefs and discourses, producing new syncretic formulations. But it was not Judaism alone that was modified, for Judaism also influenced the cultural life of the Roman Empire. In those days Judaism was a widely proselytizing religion. During the period of the Second Temple, between five and ten percent of the free Roman population was Jewish or Judaizing (people who considered themselves Jews but only circumcised their sons).

With the conquests of Alexander, Hellenistic influence reached Jerusalem's elite: the *Books of the Maccabees* mention the opening of a gymnasium by the high priest, for example. After Alexander's death and the establishment of the Seleucid Dynasty — one of the three dynasties into which the Alexandrian Empire was divided — an armed revolt took place in 167 BCE when Antiochus IV (c. 215–164 BCE) began to suppress the practice of Judaism and imposed the cult of Zeus on the Temple of Jerusalem.

The revolt was led by the Jewish priest Mattathias and his Hasmonean family (who, after their leader Judas Maccabee, were also known as the Maccabees). After their victory over Antiochus, they took control of Jerusalem and the Temple. The Maccabean triumph was possible because the Seleucid Dynasty was undergoing internal decline, and there was a geopolitical vacuum in the region because of the weakening of neighboring kingdoms.

The Hasmonean victory gave rise to the festival of Chanukah, which commemorates the miracle in which a small amount of sacred oil burned for eight days, keeping the internal flame illuminated in the recently reconquered Temple. The *Hanukia* (an eight-branched candlestick) and the Menorah (a seven-branched candlestick) represent the principle symbols of Judaism. The Star of David became associated with Judaism in the medieval period as a Kabbalistic talisman. Later its meaning changed again, as it became a decorative motif in Jewish buildings and Judaica, and then took on a national identity during and after the Holocaust — as a badge in Europe and as the flag of Israel.

The Hasmonean Dynasty (140 BCE–37 BCE) invaded new territories and converted its subjected people, but its expansion stopped at the biblical borders corresponding to the land of Israel at the time of Solomon. The Hasmonean Dynasty rapidly fell under the influence of Hellenistic culture, and its new kings were given Greek names. Finally, they were defeated by Rome, the new Mediterranean world power, which put an end to Jewish political autonomy in the land of Israel for two thousand years.

Internal divisions multiplied in Israel under the Hasmonean Dynasty and even more so in the subsequent Roman period. Flavius Josephus claims that dissident Jews called for Roman intervention because they were dissatisfied with the Hellenistic influence on the Hasmonean kings. The era's most important internal division was between the

Sadducees and the Pharisees, representing the elite priests and the urban literate class. The Sadducees took a literal approach to the Bible, whereas the Pharisees (the founders of rabbinic Judaism, which produced the Talmud) supported interpretations that went far beyond a literal rendition of the text. Thus, for instance, the Sadducees upheld the *Lex Talionis* (the law of retaliation: "an eye for an eye"), but the Pharisees proposed the payment of fines instead. Both shared contempt for the uneducated rural population (the *am ha'aretz*—literally, "the people of the land").

Each movement fought for its legitimacy inside the Great Sanhedrin (the Jewish Supreme Court), which was dominated by priests but in which the Pharisees also took part. With the destruction of the Second Temple, the Sadducees disappeared, and the Great Sanhedrin came under Pharisaic control. We know very little about the Sadducees, and what we do know comes from unfavorable sources. They were sympathetic to the Hellenistic world but objected to notions such as the immortality of the individual soul and the existence of another world. Due to foreign influence, these ideas were popular, but they were not supported by the biblical text. The Pharisees accepted this new belief system and integrated it into Judaism, making it a central component of the Talmudic tradition (which will be discussed in the next chapter). These major currents coexisted with various other religious sects and radical political groups such as the Zealots and the Sicarii, who led the great revolt against Rome that culminated in the destruction of the Second Temple.

These organized groups were generally of cultured urban origins. Unlike them, the *am haaretz*, the Jewish rural masses—strapped by poverty and suffocated by Roman taxes—were constantly stirred up by charismatic leaders who had apocalyptic and mystical tendencies—all part of the *esprit de l'époque*. Out of this context emerged the followers of Jesus of Nazareth.

The separation of the followers of Jesus from Judaism was a long and complex process in which Paul (Saul) of Tarsus played a central role. It was a practical move as well as a theological one. Still, the New Testament follows the tradition of the Pharisees in that it supports and legitimizes the veracity of its affirmations by citing passages from the biblical text. According to the New Testament, the fundamental shift occurred when the Apostolic Council of Jerusalem decreed that new converts to Christianity need not be circumcised. From a theological perspective, components of Gnosticism and Zoroastrianism (dualistic Middle Eastern religions) were increasingly integrated into Christianity, which came to emphasize the fight between good and evil, spirit and flesh, and individual salvation over the messianic vision of collective redemption.

During the Greco-Roman period, Judaism created new institutions as an alternative to the lyceum, such as the *Beit Knesset* (the synagogue—literally, "house of assembly") and the *Beit Midrash* (the study hall—literally, "house of interpretation"). Although we have insufficient information about how these institutions developed, it appears that the *Beit Knesset* was originally a substitute for the Temple in the Babylonian exile. It was a place of prayer where the Torah was read on Saturdays, but as its name implies, it was also a place of assembly. The *Beit Midrash* was founded, in the period immediately following the destruction of the Second Temple, as a place for study and biblical interpretation. Later, it became a seminary for high-level religious studies and rabbinic ordination.

Hellenistic values influenced the Diaspora communities. Philo (b. 20 BCE) of Alexandria, an Egyptian city that had a large Jewish population, read the Bible through the lens of Greek philosophical stoicism. Like the Pharisees, he placed interpretation before literal textual meaning. However, his interpretation followed a distinct path. According to Philo, God used allegories to communicate with humans. Philo argued that these allegories could be interpreted via the categories of Greek philosophy.

The Greco-Roman world favored diversity, including within Judaism, with each divergent movement confronting and interacting with others in an open manner. Tolerance for religious diversity ended only when the Roman Empire embraced Christianity. By that time, however, Pharisaic influence had gained ascendancy in the form of Talmudic Judaism, which would remain dominant within Judaism until modern times.

Talmudic Judaism

Rabbinic exegesis of the Bible became the dominant strain of Judaism, but not without opposition. Its main opponents were the Sadducees, the priestly group, and the *Apikorsim* (literally "followers of Epicurus" — in the Talmud sometimes conflated with the Sadducees). In the Middle Ages, the Karaite movement, a group that rejected the Talmud's sacredness and valued individual interpretation of the Bible, represented an important segment of the Jewish people.

The triumph of Pharisaism is often presented as a demonstration that rabbinic Judaism was the only possible and authentic path for Judaism to follow. This is an *a posteriori* construction. Pharisaic Judaism triumphed because of a series of external historical circumstances. The destruction of the Temple eliminated priestly competition, since the priests had been the legitimate holders of power. Jewish tradition was completely transformed only when the Temple was destroyed and most of the Jewish population lived outside the land of Israel. The Christianization of the Roman Empire increasingly isolated Judaism and created the conditions for Pharisaic hegemony. The tendency toward externally imposed isolation had strong affinities with the rabbinic version of

Judaism, which led Jews to inhabit a self-referential world. In modern times, when the walls of the exterior world started to crumble, so did the control of rabbinic Judaism.

The primary reference work of rabbinic Judaism is the Talmud. It comprises two conjoined sets of books, the Mishnah and the Gemarah. Whereas the Mishnah interprets the biblical text, the Gemarah reads the Bible in relation to Mishnaic interpretation. The final version of the Mishnah, written in Hebrew around 200 CE, is made up of six volumes that contain the memory of several centuries of orally transmitted traditions.

There are two versions of the Gemarah. The Jerusalem version was compiled around the end of the fourth century CE, and the Babylonian version was compiled at the beginning of the sixth century CE. They were written in different dialects of Aramaic-Hebrew. The Babylonian Gemarah is the dominant version.

The legitimacy of the Talmudic text was based on the idea that there were two types of Torah: the Torah *shebikhtav* (the written Torah—the actual biblical text) and the Torah *shebalpeh* (the oral Torah—the interpretations of those texts that were compiled in the Talmud and other writings). The relationship between the two Torahs has been the subject of constant debate, and it is the major point of division among the various denominations of contemporary religious Judaism. The key issue concerns the legitimacy of the oral tradition, which has been expanded and reinterpreted repeatedly and whose authors have added strictures, as law, to the original Torah laws.

The Talmud affirms the divine origin of the Torah (Pentateuch): it was received by Moses from God and justifies its own legitimacy in three different ways. In one version, it argues that Moses was given the Torah and the subsequent rabbinic interpretations, the Torah *shebalpeh*. A different explanation tells us that God gave Moses the rules for interpreting the written Torah, from which the rabbis drew up the new Torah. Finally, a third version, on which much of the Talmudic argument is de facto constructed, appeals to a direct relationship between the original biblical text and the new interpretations. To the question "How do we know this?" — that is, that the new interpretations are correct — the rabbis answer by citing a biblical passage to sustain their arguments.

Confidence in the correctness of the rabbis' interpretation of the biblical text was such that the Talmud includes anecdotes in which God expresses his position on controversies related to questions of purity/impurity and the rabbis ask him not to interfere.

The rabbis developed a series of reading methods — by deduction, generalization and analogy — through which they posited biblical interpretations that were not apparent. The Talmud, therefore, is based on interpretation (*drash*), the art of eliciting from the text that which does not readily appear in a literal reading (*pshat*). Under the supposition that the Torah represents the divine word, the rabbis made use of repetition, verbiage, and merged letters (in particular the letter *vav*, which is generally used as a conjunction equivalent to "and") to justify their new rules.

They also used reading methods that permitted them to relate or fuse words and phrases in order to present their interpretations as being implicit in the biblical text: for example, if one of the commandments appears twice, it can be deduced that this is not a simple repetition, because God would not speak in vain; the repetition, therefore, indicates a new meaning. In some cases it is recognized that the interpretation originates in tradition and/or rabbinical authority (*mi-de-rabbanan*) and has no basis in the written Torah. As such, the biblical support text is considered to be a simple *asmachta*, meaning that the verse is cited only as a "support" for the rule, whose source is not actually found in the Torah.

Many Talmudic rules are the product of traditions that were developed through daily practice; rabbinical reasoning, however, bestowed on them the force of law, and they became part of a closed and unchangeable system. In short, human traditions and imaginative biblical interpretations were made into sacred commandments.

The rabbis built "fences within fences" around the Torah in order to safeguard the commandments and assure that they were not transgressed. An example is the commandment that ordains, "Do not cook a kid in its mother's milk." After various "fences" were created, the rabbis decided that eating any type of meat with dairy products was prohibited. And so it came to be that when eating meat, one had to wait a number of hours before eating dairy foods. The length of time was determined by the local culture—some Jewish communities in Europe waited three hours, while others waited six.

Similar developments occurred in relation to the *Shabbat*, the day of rest. The Torah prohibits physical labor, and the rabbis stretched the notion of labor and created myriad prohibitions, including carrying items outside enclosed areas.

They translated Temple worship and priestly duties into Jewish ritual and liturgy. Prayer three times a day, and five times on the Sabbath and other holy days, replaced the cult of sacrifice, and the liturgy commemorated those sacrifices. God was blessed and thanked for food on the table, water for the crops, a good harvest, and so forth.

Following some very general indications in the Bible, the Talmud worked out most of the symbolic and liturgical apparatus that we today identify as religious Judaism. Thus, the way in which Jews celebrate the holidays, the prayers, the blessings, the rites of passage, the use of phylactery, or the criteria by which someone is said to be Jewish, date back to the Talmud.

In addition to its religious aspects, the Talmud is a code of civil law and tort law. Like most legislation originating in the Middle East, it refers to specific cases and concrete situations from which more general jurisprudence is derived. The rabbis detailed and developed laws in relation to judgments and civil and commercial rights, and they reinterpreted the *Lex Talionis* ("an eye for an eye"), permitting material compensation rather than the physical punishment of the aggressor. The rabbis did not abandon the idea of rigorous and extreme intolerance toward those who did not obey the commandments. In contrast to the ones in the Bible, the new punishments included penalties in this world and also exclusion from the afterworld and from the world to come in the time of the Messiah.

The *Midrash Halakhah* (interpretations related to the commandments) is only one component of the Talmud. A second is the *Midrash Haggadah* (narrative interpretations) — the anecdotes, metaphors, and tales that refer to biblical passages and comment on an array of subjects, including the divine origin of the written and oral versions of the Torah; the history of Israel and the lives of the rabbis themselves; the interpretation of divine intent; the description of the world of angels and sometimes demons; the coming of messianic times; and the destiny of the lost tribes of Israel. These narratives have fed the Jewish imagination for centuries.

The *Midrash Haggadah* states that prophecy, as the expression of God's voice, has ceased. God distanced himself from Israel after the destruction of the Temple and can return only with the coming of the Messiah. The rabbis decided that God could only be understood through study of the Torah.

The world of the *Midrash Haggadah* is extremely rich and imaginative, full of creative metaphors and anachronistic superstitions. It includes moments of openness to the non-Jewish world—for example, the Seven Noachide Laws issued after The Flood. They prohibit assassination, robbery, promiscuity, blasphemy, and the eating of live animals. They are just laws that apply to all people. Non-Jews who follow these laws earn the right to participate in the world to come after the advent of the Messiah. Yet in addition to these concepts, there are places where the text promotes self-isolation and xenophobia. This richness of multiple and often contradictory points of view makes the *Midrash Haggadah* an enormous cultural resource.

Pirkei Avot (literally, "Chapters of the Fathers"), a collection of maxims containing ethical teachings, is also part of the Talmud. Among these maxims are the famous words of Hillel (first century CE): "If I am not for myself, then who will be for me? And if I am only for myself, then what am I? And if not now, when?" and, "Do not do unto others that which is hateful to you. This is the whole Torah. The rest is commentary. Go and study."

The universe of the Talmud is far removed from that of the Greco-Roman culture and Christianity that surrounded its authors. The Talmud does not possess a systematic theology or even a series of dogmatic principles or a philosophical argument about God. To the rabbis, God was present in the text of the Torah. Study of the Torah—along with prayer and observance of the commandments—was the way to be in contact with God.

In many ways Athens and Jerusalem were worlds apart. It was rational argument versus interpretation of the sacred text; freedom versus collective tradition; individual ethics versus fulfillment of the commandments. Unlike the Greek philosophers, the authors of the Talmud anthropomorphize God. This humane image of God is taken literally because the Bible declares that man was made in God's image.

One can find ethics and elements of a theology in the Talmud, but they are not presented as such. And today some commandments seem "functional" or even scientifically justifiable. For example, certain kosher laws might be justified for being healthy laws, but health reasons are not part of the rationale for Jews to obey the laws of *Kashrut*. They are obeyed because those who observe them believe they are God's commandments.

Contrary to philosophy or theology, in which arguments are advanced to attain ultimate truth, the Talmudic universe accepts multiple interpretations of a text or point. This multiplicity of interpretation generates debates and rifts among different schools of rabbinic thought.

At one point the rabbis decided that history and politics were insignificant, and so rabbinical writings do not describe in detail the lives of Jews in the Diaspora, not even when the circumstances were dramatic. Historical and social events are only relevant when they suggest themes related to the *Halakhah* (the legal rules to be observed).

Under the rabbis the Torah acquired a transcendental role and became the only vital reality, the only truth, the main resource to which Jews should turn until the arrival of the Messiah. A cyclical sense of time was reinforced through daily prayer, Sabbath rest, and annual holidays.

The political conflict between Pharisees and Maccabees and the disasters caused by the two great uprisings against Rome (the destruction of the Second Temple and the revolt against the Emperor Hadrian) led the rabbis to avoid external politics as a means of influencing the future of the Jewish people: "*Dina d'malchuta dina*," they declared (the law of the land is law).

They refused to include the *Book of Maccabees* in the biblical canon because the Maccabees were zealots who rose up against the rulers of the land (Rome). The festival of Chanukah, the celebration of the Maccabees' liberation of Jerusalem and purification of the Temple, became a commemoration not of military victory but of the "divine" miracle that permitted a cruse of oil to burn for eight days instead of one. Another example of the relegation of political activism is found in the Passover Haggadah (the text read during the festival dinner): Moses, the great political statesman who led the people out of Egypt, is named only once.

However, this did not mean that Jews, even in the Middle Ages, did not have "political reach." But politics was important only because it played a pragmatic role in placating local rulers to ensure the protection and prerogatives of the Jewish community—in short, it was politics without transcendental meaning.

The Talmud portrayed Judaism as a self-contained universe, removing temporality and worldly events. This world is very distant from that of the biblical text, in which the people and their culture are constructed vis-à-vis political struggles and the passage of time. As historical experience lost its relevance to self-understanding in the framework of Talmudic thought, innovations were justified in the name of tradition rather than as adjustments to a changing social reality.

From a contemporary perspective, for some, Talmudic Judaism may appear ossified and dogmatic. Yet this is an anachronistic view, a reaction against Talmudic Judaism as it is practiced today; this view loses sight of Talmudic Judaism's originality, creativity, and vitality. Talmudic Judaism served as a survival guide for a people politically and existentially dominated. The Jews believed they were condemned to live as an exiled minority culture in the Diaspora until the coming of the Messiah.

Talmudic culture, sometimes unintentionally, did produce a psychological, practical, and cognitive universe that continues to influence contemporary Judaism. Jews reached high levels of male literacy in old Hebrew prior to modern times because of the high value placed on studying the Torah and Talmud and the use of prayer books. In communities where erudition inspired great respect, academic excellence was a path to social mobility. The complexity of rabbinic biblical study, which emphasized students' ability to analyze problems and provide new interpretations that went beyond explicit textual meaning, and promoted intellectual individualism in the context of a strong collective belief in the Torah as a guide to life.

Competitive academic excellence in the study of the Talmud in the yeshiva system and the weekly community gathering in the local synagogue inspired a strong sense of community, intellectual acumen, initiative, and personal creativity (albeit framed within a rigid system of belief). These were highly valued traits and are still reflected, in many ways, in modern Jewish communities.

Talmudic Judaism also defined a common lifestyle that unified all social classes. Shared values of charity and compassion, religious ideas and ideals, identical community institutions in every town and hamlet, and the shared fate of a nation surrounded by hostile forces and persecution diminished social distances and created great social cohesion. Despite inequalities between rich and poor, educated and uneducated—albeit enormous—Talmudic Judaism did not have a caste system like the those in Christian and Muslim societies of the Middle Ages.

After the destruction of the Temple, the priests (*cohanim* and *leviim*) lost their privileges, except the right to be the first called upon to bless the Torah during intervals in the public Torah reading. However, they were still held to the requirement to obey stringent rules of purity. For example, priests were prohibited from marrying a divorced woman because if the Messiah came and the Temple were reconstructed, the priesthood would be reinstituted; therefore, they would have to keep their "purity" in order to fulfill their duties as soon as it happened.

The demands placed on the bodies and minds of those observing h*alakhic* Judaism generated the kind of discipline and emotional and physical self-control that is generally thought to be a trait only of modern times. These ingrained collective characteristics were important factors in facilitating social ascent once Jews were permitted to participate in all professions—especially in societies where literary culture was reserved for the elite and the masses were beset by high rates of illiteracy and cultures of subordination and resignation.

The Talmudic World in the Middle Ages

Until modern times, Talmudic Judaism maintained its unity despite diasporic dispersion and the absence of a central authority. It had its internal divisions and tensions, but changes within rabbinic

Judaism were made, fundamentally, at the margins. Although the Talmud was itself a product of enormous innovation, it also created mechanisms to close down the possibility of deeper questioning. The Talmudic tradition gave precedence to the interpretations of older generations over subsequent ones and thereby created a standard of legitimization that left very little room for real innovation. If the Talmud transformed the *pshat* (basic text) into *drash* (interpretation), the later rabbinical universe transformed the new *drash* into *pshat*, treading a narrow path until the advent of modernity.

There were problems. Foremost among them was the issue of deciding which interpretation among the various rabbinical schools should be followed. Two main schools predominate in the Talmud, one led by Hillel and the other by Shammai. Whereas the school of Shammai emphasizes maximum rigor in the observance of the commandments and the meting out of punishment, the vision of the school of Hillel is more tolerant. The *Halakhah* (religious law) follows the school of Hillel.

The rabbis or rabbinical synods resolved new problems by issuing new legislation (for instance, they prohibited polygamy when surrounded by a Christian culture that did not approve of it). Certain situations required that the legal code be modified in ways that were only tenuously supported by the Talmudic text—for example, the expansion of economic activities in the sixteenth century, which created new credit instruments and modified the rules relating to loans and commerce that could be carried out with non-Jews.

Centuries of small changes generated a constant accumulation of laws and rites that needed to be organized and systemized. In the sixteenth century, Rabbi Joseph ben Ephraim Caro compiled the *Shulkhan Arukh*, the standard code of law based on the *Halakhah*. However, legal compilation efforts continue to this day.

In addition to new interpretations of those laws, different *minhagim* (customs) evolved in relation to the celebration of rites and the organization of prayer books. For the most part, these customs reflected different local traditions. The most important distinction was between the Sephardim (associated with the Muslim world and Spain and Portugal — which until the fifteenth century had part of their territories under Islamic rule) and the Ashkenazim (associated with Christian Europe).

The Sephardim and Ashkenazim created their own traditions of Talmudic study. In the Christian world, Jews were subject to constant massacres and persecution by a medieval culture that embraced belief in magic and manifested mystical and ascetic tendencies. As a consequence, European Judaism closed in upon itself. It was not immune, however, to the surrounding culture's superstitions and ascetic practices, which also became popular among Jews.

Rabbi Shlomo Yitzhaki, or Rashi (1040–1105 CE, b. Troyes, France), was among the greatest rabbis of that era. Rashi wrote comprehensive commentaries on the Bible and Talmud, commentaries that are still included in most editions of these religious texts.

The most innovative figures of Talmudic Judaism came from the Sephardic world, particularly from Spain. Periods of great openness and tolerance in Spain under Muslim rule permitted Jewish intellectuals to engage in explicit cross-cultural dialogue. Many of these authors wrote in Judeo-Arabic (Arabic written in Hebrew script) and were influenced by Greek philosophy and new linguistic techniques. Solomon ibn Gabirol (Solomon ben Judah), an Andalusian Hebrew poet and Jewish philosopher of the eleventh century, explored Neoplatonism. Rabbi Moses ben Jacob ibn Ezra, of Granada, carried out the first linguistic study of the Bible and wrote poetry that renewed the Hebrew language. Some of his poems are recited on Rosh Hashanah and Yom Kippur.

The most emblematic figure of this period is Maimonides, the Rambam (Rabbi Moses Ben Maimon—in Arabic, Abu Imran Mussa bin Maimun ibn Abdallah al-Qurtubi al-Israili), who lived between 1135 and 1204 CE and was born Córdoba, Spain. His family fled to the south and later to Morocco when the Almohad Dynasty conquered part of Spain and put an end to religious tolerance. In addition to being a well-read philosopher, he was considered one of the most distinguished medieval doctors of his time, and in the final decades of his life, established himself in Egypt as personal physician to Saladin (1138–1193 CE), the sultan of Egypt and Syria.

Maimonides wrote many books, including the *Mishneh Torah*, a compendium of rabbinical law that continues to be a major reference work. In *The Guide for the Perplexed*, Maimonides works out a synthesis of Judaism and Greek philosophy and yet defends the biblical version when it is contradicted by Aristotelianism. He opposes an anthropomorphic view of God, which opens the door to idolatry, and in accordance with Neoplatonic philosophy argues that God can be defined only by his negative attributes (what God is not). As a rationalist, Maimonides sought to diminish the importance of mysticism. He describes the coming of the Messiah as an essentially political event, related to reconstructing the reign of David in the land of Israel and characterized by charity, compassion, and peace among the peoples of the earth.

It took many centuries for his work to become widely accepted in the Jewish world. In the Middle Ages, particularly in Christian Europe, many rabbis even banned the reading of *The Guide for the Perplexed*. However, Maimonides was widely recognized by philosophers of the era, including Thomas Aquinas. With the arrival of modernity, Maimonides became known as a pioneer, a follower of the Talmud who was in dialogue with philosophy and supported the study of the natural world.

In the Muslim world, rabbinic Judaism also confronted Karaism — a religious movement initiated in Mesopotamia in the eighth century CE — which held the Bible to be the only sacred text in the canon. According to the Karaites, the Talmud contained commandments that although produced by learned individuals and tradition did not have the same force as the biblical commandments. It sought to return to the original text and promoted direct interpretation by each individual. There is still a population of around 30.000 Karaites, most of them living in Israel.

The need to respond to the Karaites and defend the Talmud obliged Jewish thinkers to revisit the traditional arguments about the Talmud's legitimacy. Thus, Saadia Gaon (882–942 CE, b. Fayum, Egypt) stressed that the Talmud was based on tradition and was needed to fill gaps in the biblical text. Judah HaLevi and Abraham ibn Ezra (ninth/tenth century CE, both born in Tudela, Spain) embraced a similar position. Although they qualified the claim that rabbinical exegesis was an expression of divine intent, they also asserted that these interpretations upheld the biblical tradition.

Maimonides, too, did not feel comfortable with the argument that the Talmud possessed the same status as the Bible, particularly when it presented conflicting interpretations. For Maimonides, God would not have produced various versions of the same subject. Maimonides concluded that laws resulting from exegesis were *mi-de-rabbanan*, products of tradition as explained by the rabbis. This did not mean that they should be disobeyed, but Maimonides felt that they could not be placed on the same level as the biblical text.

Thus, in a context in which Judaism was influenced by external cultures and confronted by opposition movements like Karaism, the rabbis formulated new justifications for the legitimacy of the Talmudic text. In the medieval world it was possible to cite tradition as an absolute value with the force of law. However, in modern times, citing tradition as a rationale for the law became insufficient as a basis for its validation.

Along with the development of Talmudic study, Judaism developed the Kabbalah, a mystical current. The principal inspirational text of the Kabbalah is contained in the apocalyptic prophecies of Ezekiel, where God appears on a throne mounted on a carriage pulled by four animals. The Kabbalah studies the attributes of God, the creation of the universe, and the conditions under which the Messiah will come. Since God cannot be known in his essence, being infinite, the Kabbalah examines his emanations as an expression of the divine attributes (*sephirot*). And since Hebrew numbers are represented by letters of the alphabet, Kabbalists follow the tradition, already present in the Talmud, of interpreting biblical words and texts based on the numerical value assigned to the letters.

In the Talmudic tradition there are four levels of biblical interpretation: *Pshat* (the simple text, the literal dimension), *Remez* (what the text suggests, the allusive dimension), *Drash* (the interpretive dimension), and *Sod* (the secret, mystical dimension).

The four initial letters of these words form the acronym PARDES, meaning "orchard."

In Talmudic Judaism the mystical dimension is traditionally approached with great reticence and was not generally permitted to be studied by young people, because it could supposedly lead to madness or apostasy.

In the sixteenth century, study of the Kabbalah was revived in Tsfat, a city in the Galilee, then under the rule of the Ottoman Empire. New Kabbalistic teachings inspired major social movements in the sixteenth and seventeenth centuries, including the messianic movement of Shabbetai Zvi and Hasidism. The principal figures responsible for this revival were Rabbis Isaac Luria and Chaim Vital (the latter edited the teachings of the former). At the heart of the Lurianic interpretation, the creation of the world is presented as God's contraction or withdrawal (*tzimtzum*). God's contraction is described as a process by which he vacated space; in the remaining emptiness, still populated by divine sparks, the universe emerged.

The exact meaning of God's contraction was, and continues to be, a subject of debate within Orthodox communities, particularly because it can give rise to a pantheistic interpretation (that is, it could be understood that there is no separation between God and the universe). Several authors saw a parallel between this version of the creation of the universe, the traumatic expulsion from Spain, and the search for a transcendental explanation for the Diaspora.

Just as the Jews were exiled from their homeland, God exiled himself in order to create the world.

The new mysticism was a response to the frustration and disenchantment caused by the Inquisition and expulsions from Spain and Portugal and the massacre of tens of thousands of Jews in Ukraine by the Cossack leader Bogdan Chmielnitzki in 1648 to 1649.

In the seventeenth century in Smyrna, Turkey, Shabbetai Tzvi (1626–1676), a young rabbi influenced by Kabbalistic teachings, proclaimed himself to be the new Jewish Messiah. He gained adherents among rabbis and power brokers in the many cities he visited in the Ottoman Empire. When he began to violate the *Halakhah*, he justified his actions by appealing to those passages in the Talmud that stated that many commandments would be abolished in messianic times. In the end, along with some of his followers, he converted to Islam.

It was not only the Ottoman Empire that felt the impact of Shabbetai Tzvi's activities. He generated an enormous wave of support for himself throughout Europe. Synagogues included prayers to praise him, and many Jews sold their belongings in preparation for their return to Israel. With its founder's conversion to Islam, the movement lost its influence, although small groups of his followers continued to exist until the twentieth century. After his death, other false Messiahs emerged and claimed to be his reincarnation.

The most influential of these was an eighteenth-century Ukrainian Jew, Jacob Frank. In the end, he converted to Catholicism. For the followers of these sects, religious conversion and transgression of the commandments were seen as ways to accelerate the coming of messianic times.

During the eighteenth century, the founding of Hasidism profoundly affected Judaism. Its founder was Rabbi Yisrael ben Eliezer (1698–1760), known to all as the *Baal Shem Tov* (literally, "Master of the Good Name").

The *Baal Shem Tov*, influenced by the Lurianic Kabbalah, argued that God was continuously present in the world and within each person. In his view, each person had the potential to recuperate a divine dimension; hence, we should be tolerant of sinners. Since divinity continues to exist in the world — even when Jews are exiled — the universe will continue to evolve until the coming of the Messiah.

Hasidism opposed the ascetic vision of the original Kabbalah. It emphasized messianic hope and expressed it through the joy of living and the pleasures offered by a life lived in obedience to the basic commandments. One could worship God with love, feelings, prayer, and song to achieve ecstatic communion with God. From this outlook, it followed that intention (*kavanah*) and emotion, more than study, would open the path to contact with God. The *Baal Shem Tov* and his disciples used stories and parables to transmit their messages. Often taken from popular, regional folklore rather than erudite exegesis of biblical texts or the Talmud, many of these stories are beautiful and filled with moral strength.

The miracles later attributed to the *Baal Shem Tov* and the heirs of the movement, in addition to placing value on simple residents of the small villages in the Pale of Settlement (the region of Imperial Russia in which permanent residence of Jews was allowed), were welcomed by large portions of Eastern European Jewry, which had been greatly affected by poverty and persecution. Some authors argue that Hasidism was also favored by wealthy members of the Jewish community who wished to diminish the power of traditional rabbis.

The Hasidic movement encountered particularly strong resistance from the head rabbis of the large yeshivas, the study centers in Lithuania, though some Talmudists did support Hasidism. The leading rabbi of the era, the Gaon of Vilna (1720-1797), believed the *Baal Shem Tov*'s interpretations and those of other Hasidic *rebbes* would lead to the denial of the separation between God and the world and to the undervaluation of Talmudic study. After the death of the *Baal Shem Tov*, his disciples became Hasidic leaders (*rebbes*) who formed their own dynasties and passed their own schools of thought down from generation to generation.

The Hasidic dynasties were often named after their towns of origin or took the names of places where they served the longest. The *rebbes* became central to the lives of those who believed in them, offering advice, distributing amulets and blessings.

In Eastern Europe many of these *rebbes* had retinues who traveled among the Jewish villages receiving presents and donations from the poor, who in turn expected to be rewarded with miracles.

The Hasidic movement made important modifications to Talmudic Judaism. First of all, it created the figure of the *rebbe*, placing him above average people in his ability to communicate with God and endowing him with special powers, including the ability to perform miracles. Second, it placed the study of mysticism and messianic expectation, previously repressed by the rabbinical tradition, at the center of Judaism.

Until a generation after World War II, ultra-Orthodox Judaism was bitterly polarized between Hasidism and the Lithuanian rabbinic leaders who opposed it (the *Mitnagdim*—literally, "those who are opposed"). The conflict even led both sides to denounce one another to local authorities—a practice that was not confined to the battles between *Mitnagdim* and Hasidim, but to all groups who disagreed with each other's interpretations of the Torah.

Jews, Christians, and Muslims

Before examining the modern era, we should pause to reflect on our current perceptions of the relationship between Judaism and the cultural influences through which it evolved over the course of nearly two thousand years. In the Middle East,

Europe, and the New World, Jews lived under the hegemony of Christianity, joined later by Islam. Reexamining the way we perceive this relationship is fundamental to understanding the trajectory of Judaism in Western culture, and thus to rethinking our own vision of Judaism.

The standard model that Jews have developed in relation to Christianity (and with less intensity to Islam) is that of victim versus executioner. This vision is bolstered by a history of periodical demonization, persecution, expulsion, forced conversion, inquisition, massacre, ghetto confinement, book burning, and prohibition of both proselytization and entry into certain professions. This history was driven in particular by the Church but also by Islamic narratives that spread hatred against Jews.

This attitude was fed by a Christian theology that recognized the Bible as a sacred text and Jesus as a Jew who had preached to his own people. Faced with the Jewish refusal to recognize Jesus as the Messiah or Muhammad (c. 570–632 CE) as the Prophet, Christianity and subsequently Islam struggled to define the place of Judaism. Paul of Tarsus, like Muhammad, expressed his frustration at trying to convince Jews to follow the new version of the Bible.

Christianity produced various theological explanations in response to the Jewish rejection of Jesus; the primary explanation was that God had transferred his alliance from the Jews to his "new people." The Jewish Diaspora and the destruction of the Temple were divine punishment because the Jews refused to accept Jesus as the Messiah.

The most damaging narrative involved the transformation of Judas into a symbol of the traitorous Jew responsible for Jesus' crucifixion, a crime that would forever be a collective, eternal Jewish responsibility. The Jews, instead of the Romans, were thus accursed forever for killing Jesus. This notion was contrary to biblical law, which prohibited holding the child accountable for the sins of the father; it created a culture of hatred and anti-Semitism that has deeply infiltrated Christianity.

The aspiration of Christianity and Islam was to become the hegemonic world religion, whether through the recognition of the divinity of Christ or the prophetic role of Muhammad. For both Christianity and Islam, Judaism was, and in a way, continues to be an "other" that is not entirely different because it has a place within their own discourses. As such, it cannot be eliminated as something that is totally different, yet it remains an irritant because it cannot be absorbed. Thus, relations with Jews have always been marked by ambivalence; Judaism shares elements with these hegemonic cultures, but at the same time Jews do not accept their particular narratives.

On the other hand, Judaism has difficulty acknowledging Christianity's and Islam's contributions to Judaism itself. Jews are proud of their contributions to humankind, in particular through monotheism, the Ten Commandments, the idea of messianic redemption, and the weekly day of rest. But if it had not been for Christianity and Islam, these innovations would have remained strictly Jewish, since Judaism was fundamentally focused on itself. These Jewish innovations were disseminated throughout the world thanks to the absorption of these ideas by the two world-conquering religions.

Christianity and Islam served as conduits for Jewish contributions to global culture. Without them, the Jewish contribution to civilization as we know it would not exist, because such was not the intention of biblical or Talmudic culture. This does not diminish the fact that the original "authorial credit" for cardinal ideas disseminated by Islam and Christianity (in their own versions) belongs to Judaism.

Each faith needs to recognize the role of the other two great monotheistic religions in the formation of contemporary civilization. Though Jews pride themselves on being the first to create monotheism and though they resent the tendency of Christians and Muslims to conceal or diminish their role, they have an equally obstructed view of their own place in history.

To the extent that we can accept the great monotheistic religions as being profoundly interconnected, we can promote a less dogmatic, less fundamentalist vision of each.

Institutionalized religions, in their orthodox or fundamentalist variations, share strong authoritarian components: they do not respect other religions, and they are not open to societies founded on individual liberty, the free expression of ideas, and the right of each individual to act in accordance with his or her own conscience. When any form of religious orthodoxy—whether Jewish, Christian, or Muslim—assumes power, democracy itself is destroyed.

At the same time, there have been great advances in the Catholic Church, whose integration into the modern world is a complex and as yet unfinished task. These advances include the elimination of anti-Semitic components from official theology under the leadership of John XXIII during the Second Vatican Council (1962–1965), a transformation that was influenced by the Holocaust and the indirect responsibility of the Church for having nourished anti-Semitic sentiments across Europe for more than two thousand years. There was also a movement within Catholicism itself to open a discourse on human rights and interreligious dialogue. Many relationships have also been forged with mainstream Protestant groups, though not all, and with moderate Islamic leaders.

Dialogue is fundamental to ensuring mutual respect and finding common ground without abdicating specific commitments. Dialogue should be promoted among religious leaders and also among secular intellectuals of Jewish, Christian, or Islamic persuasion. Today, for many Jews, Christians, and to a lesser degree Muslims, religion has become a cultural tradition whose meaning is not limited to formal religious institutions and the rules and dogma they attempt to impose.

Modernity: The Return of Philosophy, History, and Politics

To recap: Talmudic Judaism was successful as a religious institution under certain historical circumstances—when Jews were isolated within societies ruled by political and cultural systems associated with the hegemonic religions of Christianity and Islam. The closing of Judaism upon itself was linked to the way surrounding societies cut Jews and Judaism out of their communities. The Talmudic world was born of political and military defeat; the rabbis' worldview served as a survival strategy for an exiled people, a minority population living in the heart of the Diaspora.

But by the eighteenth century, Judaism had been penetrated by Enlightenment philosophy, scientific argumentation, and a view of history as the product of human action rather than the result of a divine plan. These influences caused Judaism to fragment into diverse currents. In a long historical process, secular and religious intellectuals began to introduce the values and ideas of modernity into Judaism.

Modernity brought new demands and opportunities that would cause the rabbinical universe to implode when the three elements that had been repressed by Talmudic Judaism—history, politics, and philosophical freethinking—returned to the scene.

Modern Judaism corresponds to the historical period that ran from the Enlightenment and the French Revolution until the Holocaust and the creation of the State of Israel. This period of approximately two centuries was shaped by the universalist values of the Enlightenment and the revolutions that toppled monarchal rule first in the colonies of the New World and then in France. As a sociocultural phenomenon, modern Judaism was largely a creation of metropolitan European Jews in Berlin, Vienna, Vilna, Warsaw, Budapest, Kiev, and later New York, Tel Aviv, and Jerusalem. For most Jews who lived in the Muslim world, participation in modern societies came via forced massive emigration to Israel and France in the 1950s.

The modern era created a new context of interaction between Jews and non-Jews in secular polities. This radically transformed the possibilities of Jewish social participation and simultaneously modified the Jewish vision of the meaning of Judaism. This does not imply that the relationship between Judaism and modernity was not extremely troubled on both sides. Initially, with the end of the Middle Ages and the rise of absolutism in Western Europe, the centralization of political power and the tendency toward cultural homogenization led to the expulsion of Jews from many countries, resulting in their dislocation to Central and Eastern Europe—as well as to the Netherlands and the New World.

With the advent of mercantilism, Jews were able to return to France and England in small numbers. In Western Europe, only Italy, which was divided into small kingdoms, and Holland, which had experienced two hundred years of republican government, received some of the Jews expelled from the Iberian Peninsula. Dutch Jews accompanying the Dutch West India Company during its invasion of Brazil in the seventeenth century constructed a synagogue in Recife. When they fled the Portuguese, they were set upon by pirates, had to stop in Curaçao, and then continued to the Dutch West India settlement of New Amsterdam (present-day New York), arriving in 1654. Before long, the Jews of New York had built a synagogue and imported a mohel (the man who performs circumcisions) and a kosher butcher from Palestine to serve their tiny community of fewer than thirty people.

The medieval world was subject to the will and beliefs of religious institutions. Kings ruled by the grace of God, and knowledge was produced, filtered, and censored by the clergy (or in the case of Judaism, the rabbis). Enlightenment philosophy promoted individual autonomy and the use of reason and scientific knowledge based on experimentation and hypothesis rather than religious dogma. In a long historical process, secularization separated politics from religion and transferred the source of legitimate power to the people—that is, to individuals who had the personal freedom to make free moral and political choices.

Conformity to the expression of Divine Will was replaced by belief in the human capacity to transform the world. Modern society valued liberty and the individual's right to act in accordance with his or her conscience. This process culminated in the creation of democratic institutions meant to assure that each individual, regardless of personal beliefs, could enjoy the same rights and responsibilities before the law and in the public sphere.

The Enlightenment and the French Revolution found the Jewish population severely weakened. In 1700, the world Jewish population numbered one million souls, one of the lowest in its history. A great number of these Jews lived in poverty in Eastern Europe, deprived of the right to move from place to place and beset by constant discrimination.

Modernity created tremendous conflict within the Jewish community, pitting defenders of tradition against proponents of change; often, this conflict was intergenerational. However, the impressive predisposition of most Jews to adopt new values was based on the centuries of oppression and humiliation that had preceded the Enlightenment. Modernity emerged in Jewish life as a promise of freedom, and some Jews saw Napoleon as a harbinger of the Messiah.

Most of all, modern culture did not require Jews to convert to another religion in order to absorb new ideas and values, though this was not exactly the case in Germany and the Austro-Hungarian Empire. Jews who came in contact with modern values could escape from the ghetto, obtain access to previously forbidden professions, and above all actively participate in the construction of a world where all human beings were free and equal. All of this was possible without having to abandon Judaism.

This journey continues to be a painful one because Enlightenment values required deep transformations in Judaism and the broader society. It is a tortuous path fraught with periodic and often dramatic episodes of virulent anti-Semitism, as in the case of Nazism and the Holocaust. Anti-Semitic recalcitrance produced an internal conflict between the will to believe in modernity's promise and the fear that the nightmare of anti-Semitism would always return.

Despite rabbinical opposition, modern values penetrated both daily life and the minds and hearts of Jewish individuals. This process diluted the isolation of Jewish communities, which were normally under the strong control of the rabbis, who litigated civil, commercial, and religious law.

Everywhere, depending on local conditions, there were masses of Jews who absorbed the values of modernity and distanced themselves from the world of the Talmud. At the beginning of the nineteenth century, new forms of secular and religious leadership appeared, culminating in a major change in the twentieth century when Orthodox rabbis were no longer regarded as the principal cultural elite within Judaism.

The Enlightenment's philosophy, scientific argumentation, and vision of history as a product of human action penetrated Judaism and caused its fragmentation into diverse currents. During a long historical process, secular and religious intellectuals began to incorporate the values and ideas of modernity into Judaism.

The key author of the transition to this new form of Judaism was Baruch Spinoza (1632–1677), who lived in Amsterdam and faced a community solidly controlled by Jewish Orthodoxy. The institutional and cognitive closed-mindedness of Orthodoxy led him to reduce Judaism to an anachronistic religion.

Spinoza and another heretical writer in Amsterdam, Uriel Acosta (1585–1640), focused on the Talmud's limitations and the Bible's human origin. Both were descendants of *Conversos*, children of Portuguese Jews who had been forced to convert to Christianity; both embraced a worldview in which all religious dogma, whether Jewish or Christian was narrow and irrational. Both men developed philosophical views that advocated religious tolerance and rationality.

In his primary work, the *Theological-Political Treatise*, Spinoza concludes that the Bible was a human creation written by multiple authors. He finds part of its content unacceptable and offensive to morality. Moses was not the voice of God, he argues, but a statesman who provided the Jewish people with a constitution. According to Spinoza, if human beings wrote the Bible, it should be understood in a straightforward, literal sense and should not be treated as an expression of the "Divine Word" containing various hidden meanings. He argues that belief in a deeper meaning created a regime of truth in service to the power and ambition of the clergy and the rabbis. Spinoza sought to break the rabbis' monopoly on biblical interpretation and dedicated the final years of his short life to working out a Hebrew grammar that would allow everyone to understand the meaning of the biblical text.

The price paid by Spinoza for his daring move was a form of excommunication known as *cherem*. *Cherem* prohibits an expelled person from any contact with members of the community. Uriel Acosta suffered a similar fate but tried to return to the communal fold, an effort that involved being humiliated. After writing a memoir denouncing this intolerance, Acosta committed suicide.

Spinoza and Acosta were pioneers of a movement characteristic of modernity that involved Jewish intellectuals, artists, scientists, and politicians whose work was directed toward a broader public, independent of religious belief. In this way, Jews became divorced from Judaism; that is, the Jewish origins of an author did not imply that his or her work would be limited to Jewish issues or based solely upon the tenets of Judaism—although an author's cultural roots might exert a greater or lesser degree of influence on his or her reflections.

The most important vehicle for the transmission of Enlightenment values was the creation of the nation-state, which, through the notion of citizenship, created a new category of people who were equal before the law regardless of their personal beliefs. But Europe's nation-states did not arise from a cultural tabula rasa. They were built upon preexisting Christian cultural traditions. Neither the integration of Jews into the modern state nor the acceptance of Jews as equals was ever automatic or complete.

This fear of being excluded as alien by the majority culture continues to affect the Jewish psyche. In the Americas, however, during the last century, this feeling was more intense among first generation immigrants than it is among their descendants.

The rise of the modern state posed the problem of how to emancipate Jews who until then had lived under the special protection of the king. But the transformation of Jews into citizens, even for the defenders of the Jewish cause, was not simple. During the French Revolution those supporting the political emancipation of the Jews expected that it would also emancipate them from Judaism. They believed that Judaism included "vices" such as "repulsive and misanthropic eating habits," which were explained as an effect of the isolation to which the Jews had been condemned. The so-called Philosemites argued that integration into society would allow for the rapid "regeneration" of the Jews.

Oriented by an evolutionary vision that gave primacy to Western Christian civilization, philosophers of history, from Georg Wilhelm Friedrich Hegel (1770–1831) to Oswald Arnold Spengler (1880–1936), considered the survival of Judaism an aberration. For them, Judaism had lost its raison d'être after completing its historical role during the biblical period. Josef Stalin (1878-1953) proposed a different version of this view when he argued that Jews lacked a fundamental characteristic that would make them a nation—namely, a common territory. The consequence was that the Jews and Jewish intellectuals, in particular, became obliged to respond to a double demand: that of absorbing modern values while justifying the continuity of Judaism. How could they continue to be Jews and yet be faithful to the national state and/or universal human values? All definitions of modern Judaism have been offered in answer to this question.

Napoleon Bonaparte (1769-1821), the great architect of the modern French state, explicitly put forth the problem of "dual loyalty." He convened a Sanhedrin, an assembly of representatives from the French Jewish community, to respond to a series of questions that would allow him to decide whether the Jews were willing to accept the laws of the state and be faithful to the homeland.

Napoleon accepted their answers and granted the Jews status as "French citizens of the Mosaic faith," an identity that remained solid until World War II, despite the setback of the Dreyfus Affair. (Alfred Dreyfus [1859-1935], a French army captain, was condemned to life in prison in 1894 under the false allegation that he was a traitor to France—an allegation based on a forged dossier presented by his fellow officers. The fight on his behalf was led by Émile Zola, a leading French thinker, who wrote the famous letter "J'accuse," which helped free the captain but clearly indicated that the French state had not yet eliminated the reactionary and anti-republican forces of ultraconservative Catholicism.)

Despite its secular tendencies, the national state maintained continuous ties with the Christian world: the day of rest continued to be Sunday, and no changes were made to the majority of holidays or the calendar itself. There was no parallel in European history to the case of France, where the founding of a republic signaled the willingness to make a radical cut with the past, which even included, during the French Revolution, the creation of a new calendar.

Prior to World War I, most European countries were parliamentary monarchies that maintained Christian symbols as part of the official culture of the state. To varying degrees, Jews continued to be excluded from public office. Such was the case in the Austro-Hungarian Empire, the various German principalities, and the German state as designed by Bismark. In Russia, absolute monarchic power used anti-Semitism as a channel for popular resentment. In those countries, Jews could not, de facto or de jure, occupy positions of public service. This prohibition drove many Jews to convert, including Karl Marx's parents, the poet Heinrich Heine, and the composer and conductor Gustav Mahler.

Under the impact of modern values, Judaism began to fragment into diverse currents that expressed various social, religious, cultural, and political worldviews. For the generations who lived through it, this process was extremely painful, pitting parents against their children, dividing communities, and leading to mutual accusations that one side or the other was destroying Judaism. These fears were unfounded, however, and Judaism was actually reinvigorated by these confrontations.

Cultural and Political Movements in Modern Judaism

The diverse currents of modern Judaism reflect the variety of national, social, and political realities of specific European countries. Modern Judaism developed along two vectors: the religious and the political. In the religious arena, the questioning of Talmudic Judaism was centered in Germany, which had the largest concentration of Jews in Western and Central Europe. In contrast to France, whose republic had granted citizenship to the entire population, discrimination against Jews continued in Germany, first in its various principalities and then in the unified nation under the aegis of Prussia. Moreover, the constant influx of poor Jews from Eastern Europe provoked feelings of discomfort and prejudice among German Jews, who had become integrated into German culture. They looked upon these immigrants as a threat to their own acceptance by non-Jews.

The desire, therefore, to distance themselves from traditional Judaism, to absorb the values of the Enlightenment, and to be accepted by German society led the Jews of Germany, as well as those of Denmark, England, and Austria, to reform normative Judaism.

In Eastern Europe and Russia, the process of secularization followed different paths. In contrast to Central and Western Europe, where Jews were beginning to become more socially integrated, in the autocratic Russian Empire (which included Poland), citizenship was not the order of the day. In Eastern Europe, most Jews lived in poverty, with conflict breaking out between poor and rich Jews. In this context, rather than religious or cultural reform, ideologies oriented toward political and social reforms, like communism, socialism, and Zionism prevailed.

For the proponents of these ideologies, equality for Jews could be attained only by changing society as a whole or by creating a Jewish State. In Germany rabbis led the charge for change; in Eastern Europe secular intellectuals, critical of religion, came to the fore.

These two orientations, one focused on religious change and the other on promoting secular ideologies with strong political content, existed in parallel until a certain point. With the passage of time, however, they began to converge. But the relationship between political movements and religious movements has never been easy. For example, Reform Jews and Orthodox Jews, for different reasons, initially opposed Zionism (the former so as not to call their national loyalties into question and the latter because they were still attached to messianic belief).

The nineteenth century saw an explosion of belief in human progress in Europe. Continual changes confirmed that the past was different from the present and that the future was open, thus placing history at the center of the understanding of social reality. Societies were explained as products of human action, and academic historians were mobilized to serve the great ideologies of nationalism, liberalism, and socialism.

A series of intellectuals began to recount the "history of the Jewish people" based on historical documents. They unfolded a new version of Judaism as the making of a nation via history and human intervention.

Germany was the principal arena for discussion of the process through which Judaism would absorb modern values within mostly Christian societies. The questioning of traditional Judaism was centered on the legitimacy of Talmudic interpretation. Jewish intellectuals started to treat the Bible and Talmud as historical texts to which they could apply modern linguistic techniques. This allowed both texts to be viewed as the product of multiple writers and historical periods as well as differing schools of thought.

In the Talmudic text, tensions were found between the disciples of Rabbi Akiba (50–135 CE), who produced very flexible interpretations of the biblical text, and the followers of Ishmael ben Elisha (90–135 CE), who stayed closer to the original meaning. Above all, what emerged was an interpretation of the Talmud as an effort to give sacred value to innovations that were born of specific historical contexts, using exegesis of biblical texts to make them "holy."

The rabbis who produced the Talmud were seen as highly innovative intellectuals for their time. Their mistake had been to view historically dated traditions as eternal verities. Following the example of creativity set by the Talmudic rabbis would mean that the Bible should be constantly reinterpreted and updated to reflect contemporary times.

Reform Judaism was the first movement to propose radical changes in this direction. It tried to transform Judaism by eliminating most of its national content, and it targeted daily prayers, rules constructed around what is pure or impure, and the observance of the Sabbath as a day of rest.

The Reform position was that the essence of Judaism is ethics, to care for the poor, the widows, and the orphans, and its role should be to contribute to the betterment of humanity. Religious practice was changed, and men and women sat and prayed together in the synagogue, which, inspired by Protestant churches, began to enhance services with music and vernacular prayers. The effort to associate Judaism with liberal discourse and national citizenship created a rift between the Reform and the mystical and nationalist branches of Judaism. Reform Judaism gave the coming of the Messiah ethical substance and distanced itself from Zionism.

As time went on, Reform Judaism changed. In the second half of the twentieth century, it became more traditional, supported Zionism, and came to value the use of Hebrew in the liturgy. At the same time, it integrated new cultural tendencies, allowing female rabbis to practice and accepting homosexuality. Today, Reform Judaism is the primary denomination of religious Judaism in the United States, and it exists in an enormous variety of versions. Each rabbi and synagogue has its own peculiarities in accordance with the characteristics of the local community (and/or the rabbi).

The second line of religious renovation was Conservative Judaism (the name has nothing to do with political ideology but with the desire to preserve tradition and stand apart from Reform and Orthodox Judaism). Although its intellectual basis was elaborated in Germany, as a religious movement it is basically an American phenomenon which sought to combine the traditionalism of Eastern European Jewish immigrants with modern values. Believing in the divine character of the Torah, it has kept prayers in Hebrew. Though it recognizes the historical character of Talmudic innovation, it continues to view the Talmud as a central reference point. Conservative Judaism practices the commandments related to *Kashrut* (Jewish dietary laws) and the Sabbath, but with ample tolerance. In certain areas, it has made major changes — for example, it accepts the equal participation of women in religious rituals and community institutions, even consecrating them as rabbis, and seeks to embrace universal values of social justice. The Conservative movement has always supported Zionism.

For a long time, Conservative Judaism was the primary Jewish religious denomination in the United States. It functioned as an adaptive bridge between the traditional religiosity of Eastern European Jews and the New World. But in the past few decades, it has been losing ground to Reform Judaism and to a lesser degree, to a return by many to mainstream Orthodoxy.

Today, it is divided between a more conservative leadership that seeks to limit change and maintain an attachment to Talmudic tradition on the one hand and a base that is pressing for greater openness on the other. Recently it has adapted kosher laws that are determined by how a product is made — whether it is green and whether laws regarding labor, human rights, and animal rights have been adhered to. Initiated by Renewal Rabbi Arthur Waskow, the movement has caused conflict with some streams of Orthodox Jewry.

Reconstructionist Judaism, a smaller movement that oscillates between Conservative and Reform currents, was inspired by Rabbi Mordechai Kaplan (1881–1983), one of the great figures of twentieth century Judaism. In recent decades, part of the creativity of religious Judaism migrated from the great institutional centers to relatively marginal movements like Renewal, founded by Rabbi Zalman M. Schachter-Shalomi (b. 1924), the magazine *Tikkun*, published in San Francisco, and outreach organizations like Be'chol Lashon, which advocates growth and diversity among all Jewish denominations. There are also hundreds of synagogues and institutions where new interpretations of religious Judaism are being explored.

The fragmentation of religious Judaism also led to an internal division among the followers of Talmudic Judaism: between the Orthodox and the so-called ultra-Orthodox, or *Haredim*. Beginning in nineteenth-century Germany, some Orthodox Jews concluded that an effort should be made to adapt to modern life. They included scientific disciplines in school curricula; they studied at universities; and they embraced some modern lifestyles and values. Some of them also became active participants in the Zionist movement. Today, Orthodox Judaism is internally fragmented and contains different coexisting traditions. In Israel, for example, the Orthodox are divided between those from the West and those from Muslim countries.

Similar diversity and changes can also be found in the ultra-Orthodox world. Since the establishment of the Beth Jacob school system founded by Sara Schenirer in Krakow, Poland, between the World Wars, Orthodox women have been permitted to pursue formal Jewish education to become teachers of Jewish children. More recently, some have been allowed to study Talmud and law and become advocates for women in Jewish courts. Not all streams of Orthodoxy accept this, but women are slowly beginning to assert some rights, including working outside the home and obtaining a secular education that would help them provide for their families. Yet women still cannot be witnesses in court and cannot divorce a man unless he agrees to it.

The ultra-Orthodox are extremely diverse. In Israel, the *Edot HaMizrach* (Jews of the Islamic world) have distanced themselves from the hegemony of the *yeshivot*, centers for Torah study and rabbinical ordination, which are Ashkenazi in origin, and have built their own centers. There are Hasidic groups and those who oppose them, and some Hasidic sects are barely civil to one another. In general, ultra-Orthodox groups remain distant from Zionism, and there are those who do not recognize the existence of the State of Israel and will not vote, pay taxes, or serve in the armed forces, even when they live in Israel. Others participate in the political life of the country and seek to advance their interests and impose their religious vision on the state.

One different strain of Hasidism was Chabad, a Hasidic movement whose name is a compound formed from the Hebrew words *chochmah* (wisdom), *binah* (comprehension), and *da'at* (knowledge). Founded in the late eighteenth century by Rabbi Shneur Zalman of Liadi, it is also known as Lubavitch—the name of the town in White Russia where it was originally based. Today, its followers are called Lubavitchers and Chabadniks. Shneur Zalman wrote the *Tanya*, a Kabbalistic work that serves as Chabad's main reference book. It has its own interpretation of the Kabbalah and teaches that every aspect of the world exists only through the intervention of God. The *Tanya* places the "mind" in a position of control over the emotions and underscores this to set Chabad apart from other forms of Hasidism.

During the Holocaust, Chabad's sixth leader, Rabbi Yosef Yitzchok Schneersohn, fled to New York. Rabbi Menachem Mendel Schneerson, his son-in-law and successor, trained his students and sent some of them out to proselytize secular Jews on college campuses across America. With the use of marketing and hi-tech communication, the movement became a powerful force. Today it is estimated that there are 3,300 Chabad institutions in over 900 cities in 75 countries, with around 200,000 adherents (1.5 percent of the world Jewish population).

Because of Schneerson's ability to wield incredible influence over his closest followers, some of them began to testify that the "*rebbe* was *Moshiach*" (the Messiah). The belief that Schneerson was/is the Messiah has fractured even the Chabad community since his death in 1994. He had no son or appointee to replace him, and his position remains vacant. Schneerson's theology also permitted political activism in the State of Israel, an activism that is prohibited by most mainstream Hasidic leaders, who believe that a state of Israel can only be created by God in the messianic era.

Together, Orthodox and ultra-Orthodox groups constitute a minority within Judaism, 15 percent in the United States and 25 percent in Israel, where their population has grown due mainly to high fertility rates among Haredim.

Secular Jews — that is, Jews who define themselves as Jewish vis-à-vis human bonds related to biography, history, and culture, without reference to belief in sacred books — constitute the major branch within Judaism. Secular individuals and social movements seek new ways to continue to be Jewish in modern society, moving beyond religion and viewing Judaism primarily in terms of humanistic values. In the past, some have looked for answers beyond Judaism itself — via socialism, for example, which promised the redemption of humanity and the end of divisions between nations.

In the twentieth century, the two key strains of secular Judaism, the socialist Bund and Zionism, developed nationalist versions of Judaism. The Bund brought together Jewish workers in Eastern Europe, and thanks to the strong Jewish tradition of solidarity and social cohesion, became the principal social-democratic party of the Czarist Empire (Poland, the Baltic countries, and Russia) at the beginning of the twentieth century.

The Bund was based on the promotion of Yiddish culture. Yiddish, written using Hebrew letters, is a language derived from old German with a great number of borrowings from both Slavic languages and Hebrew; it served as the *lingua franca* among Eastern European Jews and beyond.

Yiddish culture was vibrant and included hundreds of theater troupes, musicians, and newspapers, as well as a film industry, a vast literary oeuvre, and editorial houses that translated an impressive number of scientific and literary works. Defending the view that the Jews were a national minority, the Bund demanded the right to cultural autonomy.

After the Russian Revolution of 1917, which imposed the dictatorship of the Communist Party and banned all other political parties, many members of the Bund in the Soviet Union become Communists. In Poland, they continued to have wide support until the Holocaust. Many Bundist immigrants, who came to America at the turn of the twentieth century, re-created the movement in North America, where they maintained schools and cultural centers and were strong participants in local politics, especially the development of workers' unions. At its peak in 1914, the Workmen's Circle (Arbeter Ring) brought together 210,000 members.

The decline of the Bund was a result of the destruction of Eastern European Jewish communities during the Holocaust and under Stalinism. In the United States there were other contributing factors, including the social mobility and cultural integration of Jews into American society. And then there was also the emergence of the State of Israel and its pro-Hebrew policy and finally the Soviet Union's turning against Israel. But in many places Bund schools and cultural centers adapted to new times, continuing to teach Yiddish and Yiddish culture. They remain an important force within secular Judaism.

Zionism, the other major current of secular Judaism, was inspired by nineteenth-century European nationalism and proposed as a solution to the problem of anti-Semitism, which the founders believed was the fundamental problem and origin of the exclusion, humiliation, and oppression of the Jews.

Created by secular Jews, Zionism rejected the idea of waiting for the Messiah to establish a Jewish homeland, and it developed a narrative regarding diasporic Judaism that characterized Jews as a minority doomed to persecution because they lacked their own territory. Zionism turned to politics as a means of redeeming the Jewish people. Its basic objective was to "normalize" the Jewish people, transforming them into a nation like all others via the establishment of a Jewish homeland in Israel.

Zionism was organized around political parties that included Marxist-Leninist groups, the Labor Party (which was the hegemonic faction), liberals, and rightwing nationalists. The historical consequences of the Zionist movement and the challenges facing secular humanistic Jews in our time will be discussed in later chapters.

To summarize, what were the main characteristics of secular Judaism in the nineteenth and twentieth centuries?

1. Jewish identity is separate from religion: this separation has never been complete, and modern Judaism has maintained ambiguous links to some traditions of Talmudic origin.

2. Secular Judaism sought to transform and legitimize Judaism vis-à-vis modern values, arguing that Judaism was capable of expressing itself in "universal" terms.

3. Secular Judaism was framed by the great ideological movements of its time such as liberalism, socialism, and nationalism—movements based on the idea that societies could be constructed out of projects that were based solely on rationality and ethics. This context created a doctrinaire, discursive, logical approach born of the desire to reconcile Judaism with modern values; this approach ignored the challenges posed by the rituals and nonrational elements associated with Jewish culture and identity.

4. On a personal level, this transformation was experienced as an identity crisis, as a divide between tradition and modernity, between loyalty to humanity and/or national society and primordial ties, between emotion and reason.

PART TWO

CONTEMPORARY JUDAISM

The Holocaust, Memory, and Politics

The Holocaust took the lives of more than six million people and destroyed major centers of religious and secular Jewish culture. It eroded the belief of many Jews in the possibility of a world guided solely by reason and created massive support for Zionism, which until then had been only one of many Jewish ideologies. It shifted the global geographical distribution of Jews, transforming the United States into the primary demographic center in the Diaspora, and it was a central influence in the creation of the State of Israel. But the most disturbing effect today is that Judaism, implicitly and explicitly, continues to live in its shadow.

The Holocaust will certainly continue to affect Jews and Judaism for a long time to come, and as with all historical traumas, overcoming it will take generations. However, the dimension it has acquired as a central point of reference for contemporary Jewish identity — often in an almost exclusive way — impoverishes collective memory.

Overcoming the Holocaust demands a tremendous effort to recover the memory of the Jewish cultural world that existed in Europe before the war. The greatest memorial one can build for those who perished is to remember the lives they lived and their richness and diversity. It is a difficult task, especially since, in Israel, the Holocaust has been transformed into a symbol of the negative dimensions of the Diaspora, while in the Diaspora, it is used primarily to transmit a sense of identification with Judaism through the "fear factor" — it happened once and can happen again.

The most profound effect of the Holocaust on the Jewish psyche was the "lesson" that the destiny of the Jews depends on their own actions and not divine intervention. After the Holocaust, independent of their belief or non-belief in God, few Jews, even among the Orthodox, continue to believe that they can depend only on God in moments of danger. In this specific sense it transformed the majority of Jews into "atheists." The Holocaust created a new alliance (from which God was excluded or at least absent) between the most diverse types of Judaism and Jews, an alliance built around memory, solidarity, and readiness for self-defense.

This positive lesson from history sometimes goes side by side with a discourse that claims that Jews are alone and have only other Jews to rely upon in moments of danger. It is a secular version of the religious narrative that insists on the importance of remembering the moments of persecution and collective suffering. This vision exists in various commemorative "holy" days, not only in recalling sad events like the destruction of the First and Second Temples but also in celebrating the most joyful of festivals, such as Purim. Purim commemorates the intervention by Queen Esther, a Jewess married to Xerxes I, the Zoroastrian king of Persia (Ahasuerus), who, by her wits, saved the kingdom's Jews from the genocide planned by Haman, the king's vizier. In conclusion, the great joy is that the Jews were saved from genocide!

This "siege mentality" is wrong from a moral and political, as well as historical, point of view. It is historically inaccurate because the Jewish people have always depended on alliances with non-Jews in order to survive. It is also morally false because it overlooks, for instance, the non-Jews who in the Second World War put their lives at risk to save Jews. Politically, it forgets, for example, that the creation of the State of Israel was possible due to a majority vote of the international community via the United Nations; indeed, the newborn state received wartime military aid from the Soviet bloc at first, then France, and finally the United States. The capacity to mobilize outside support was and continues to be one of the principal conditions for the survival of the State of Israel and the Jewish people.

Memory plays an important role in the process of our becoming social beings, but it can also become our principal source of suffering. Although memory roots us and gives us a sense of continuity as individuals and members of a community, it can also oppress us. By focusing on tragedy, and then carelessly injecting it into our children, such memories can transform learning opportunities into traumatic events, giving rise to resentment and trapping us in an improvised vision of our past.

The present cannot exist without the past, and the past is always interpreted in light of the present. In short, we create our memories, and memory is not static: people forget and people embroider; what is remembered and how it is remembered is a result of conflicting interests in every individual's psyche and even more so in the psyche—and on the political agendas—of social groups. Therefore, the preservation of memory is an exercise of power, and the strength of that power is measured by the ability to impose a specific interpretation on the meaning of the past.

The Holocaust is an exemplary case of uses and abuses in the construction of collective memories. The passage from personal suffering, lived by all who went through the Holocaust, to a narrative about its significance is not a straight line and demands constant vigilant effort and reflection.

It is a delicate and difficult exercise to discuss the question of the political uses given the Holocaust. This is especially so in light of negationist tendencies and particularly after the Iranian government's strategy of denying the Holocaust, supported by several Palestinian political organizations. This strategy attempts to delegitimize the right to existence of the State of Israel by comparing the practice of the Israeli military to that of the Nazis. Words are not naive. To dehumanize one's adversary is the first step toward justifying their destruction.

This situation produces defensive reactions that make a thoughtful discussion about the current meaning of the Holocaust difficult. But without this discussion we remain at the mercy of leaders in the Diaspora and in Israel who make use of the tragedy to justify specific political and cultural agendas.

In both cases, in Israel and in the Diaspora, a discourse has been constructed around the historical exceptionality of the Holocaust. But even if the Holocaust was unprecedented, it did set a precedent, and we should put its lessons to work in a humanistic way. Therefore, the main moral and political question is not whether it was or was not a unique phenomenon, it is about the meaning that should be drawn from this exceptionality. From a moral point of view, one-sided emphasis on the exceptional nature of the Holocaust is unsustainable because the human suffering produced by genocide is incommensurable. Politically, if the Holocaust was a historical exception, we can lament that it happened, but it is irrelevant to new generations. The Holocaust has much to teach us because in a fundamental moral sense it was not an exception but a product of hatred, intolerance, inhumanity, and the demonization of those who were different. These destructive tendencies are always present in every society. The Holocaust is a symbol, and not the only one, of the terrible consequences and destructive potential of ideologies and political regimes that sustain themselves on fanaticism and the denial of the humanity of the other.

The first task of the fight to preserve the memory of the Holocaust is to confront deniers, those who call into question the Nazi genocide or use the Holocaust for anti-Israeli political propaganda. Indeed, condemning *any use* of the Holocaust for specific partisan agendas is a condition for seeing it as a human tragedy of catastrophic proportions, so that its memory may serve as a means to uphold humanistic values.

Holocaust education can work only if it is tied to the unceasing battle against intolerance and persecution. Otherwise, in this solipsistic world, the victims of other genocides and persecutions will be thrown into a contest to determine who has suffered more. Such "competition" makes individuals look at their own suffering instead of promoting a vision that unifies all victims around humanistic ideals. We must advance a dialogue that demonstrates that the Holocaust is a phenomenon relevant not only to Jews but to all stigmatized groups and that only democratic institutions and respect for all cultures can secure the survival and dignity of minorities.

The State of Israel: The Challenge of Creating a Secular Democracy

For those who fled the pogroms of Eastern Europe and the Holocaust and still remembered, the creation of the State of Israel was an incomparable emotional experience. When I asked my father—the son of a rabbi who lost his entire family in the Holocaust—if he still believed in the coming of the Messiah, he responded that for him the birth of the State of Israel was "like the advent of the Messiah."

The State of Israel gave dignity back to a downcast generation and a people who had lived an insecure life in the Diaspora for two thousand years without any means of self-defense against external violence. The shout that rang out in the ghetto of Warsaw, "Let us not walk as sheep to the slaughter," was personified in the figure of the Israeli soldier.

The confrontation with the armies of Arab nations in the fight for independence in 1948 to 1949 resuscitated the image of David facing Goliath and of the Maccabees. The value given to working the land restored the self-image of a people whom the Diaspora had uprooted from nature. The kibbutz was a rare success story to unite collectivist communities with freedom. A democratic and egalitarian country with a workers' movement controlling an important part of the economy, agriculture sustained by cooperatives or workers' collectives, a vibrant scientific life—these all became a profound source of pride. A new socialist, secular Jewish culture promoted by the kibbutzim gave value once again to the Jewish holidays in relation to the seasons, while religious symbols gave way to a national and secular culture.

In recent decades, however, Israeli reality has changed, and many of these images have lost their force. With economic development, Israeli society acquired an urban and capitalist character, changing the agro-pastoral and secular-socialist orientation of Israeli culture. The kibbutzim underwent a major crisis, and although some have survived by adapting to their new circumstances, they are no longer icons of Israeli life. Social inequalities have increased, and internal divides and cultural fragmentation have grown deeper. In many ways Israeli democracy is still exemplary, but constant war and more than forty years of occupation have poisoned souls and affected democratic institutions, especially regarding the rights of the Arab Israeli minority and even more so the population of the territories occupied during the Six-Day War of 1967.

What happened? Israel suffered a double, mutually reinforcing crisis. On the one hand was the moral crisis produced by the occupation after the Six-Day War and on the other was the political identity crisis tied to the relation between state and religion.

From the time the Zionists settlers began to arrive in Palestine the relationship between Israel, the surrounding Arab states, and the Palestinians has never been an easy one. For the Jews it was a return to the homeland to which they had had strong religious and cultural ties for two thousand years—a land where there had always been some Jewish presence, except during periods of expulsion. Yet the Arab world saw the arrival of the Jews as a European invasion. Many Zionist leaders were insensitive to the feelings of the local population, and mutual distrust and open conflict was reinforced by Arab leaders—increasingly influenced by modern anti-Semitic literature—who announced their intent to expel the Jewish population and afterwards destroy the State of Israel.

The actions of the Israeli army were seen as legitimate and were supported for the most part by Western public opinion, so long as those actions were perceived as defending Israel's right to exist within the "green line" produced by the War of Independence. But the conquest of the West Bank, Gaza Strip, and Golan Heights during the Six-Day War led members of the Israeli government and part of the Israeli public to believe in the possibility of a "Greater Israel." The policy of building settlements in the occupied territories was initially based on the supposition that it would be possible to maintain indefinite control with the support of the United States in a world polarized by the Cold War, which no one imagined would end within the foreseeable future.

Occupation and settlements have created a tremendous moral and political dilemma for many humanistic Jews who support the State of Israel and identify with its raison d'être. They disagree with the politics of occupation but do not want to play the enemy's game, in particular when the Palestinian cause is associated with anti-Semitic positions. Although branded by some community leaders as Jews driven by self-hatred, all who oppose the occupation, whether they are in Israel or the Diaspora—without romantic illusions about the difficulties of the peace process or the intentions of many Arab leaders—serve as an integral voice for contemporary Judaism.

The moral crisis produced by the occupation has converged with and amplified another crisis related to the meaning of Jewish identity in Israel. For the Zionist pioneers and ideologues, this meaning was full of ambiguity. At its origins, Zionism was an explicit effort on the part of secular Jews to "normalize" the Jewish people. It aimed to create a national homeland that would be the safest refuge from anti-Semitism.

The Diaspora was considered an anomaly—a source of suffering that would likely disappear with the ingathering of Jews from around the world in a state inspired by the model of nineteenth-century European nationalism. In the new Jewish State a new people would emerge, free from the traumas of the past.

Zionism and the settlers of Israel sought to create a new Jewish culture on a secular basis that would erase the two thousand years in exile—represented as a purely negative period of persecutions and humiliations. The effort to create a "new man" was colossal. Zionism rejected the languages of the Diaspora and resuscitated Hebrew as the daily language (marginalizing those who preferred Yiddish or German). It developed a version of Jewish history centered on the land of Israel and the biblical period up to the Second Temple. It valued physical labor and the "return to nature."

The great majority of Zionists abandoned religion, which they blamed for the passive attitudes of Diaspora Jews who were just waiting for the Messiah to arrive. The lyrics chosen for the national anthem, *Hatikvah* ("The Hope"), do not mention God, unlike proposals to use texts taken from the Psalms.

What else happened to distance Zionism from its goal of "normalizing" the Jewish condition? Ironically, it was the impact of the Jewish immigrants who came to Israel from all corners of the world, bringing with them their different diasporic cultures.

The idea of creating a homogenized Israeli culture through a socially engineered project that did not recognize the different national cultural origins of each wave of immigrants proved unrealistic. The constant arrival of immigrants — who brought their own Jewish and national cultures, often religious and traditionalist — undermined the national secular society that the first generation of pioneers had sought to build.

Today, Israeli society reflects the mosaic of national cultures of the diverse communities of the Diaspora. Constant war with the Arabs and the need of support from Jews in the Diaspora has acted as a buffer against the development of a self-centered, "separatist" Israeli culture. Indeed, Israeli culture has always been marked by the local origins of immigrants.

The first wave of emigrants from Eastern Europe brought secularism, socialism, and music. Soon after the creation of the State of Israel, large-scale migration from Muslim countries brought traditionalist and religious values. Today, some of these groups support the political party Shas, which defends the corporate interests of this population within a conservative religious political worldview.

Similarly, the recent migration of more than a million Jews from the former Soviet Union has created a community that clings to its Russian culture. A large number of these immigrants also support their own political parties, which are religious, ultranationalist, or secular. To a greater or lesser degree, each group, including those from North and Latin America, maintains its own organizations and forms of sociability. In turn, there have been hundreds of thousands of Israelis who have left the country and returned to the Diaspora.

Israel is a young state being constantly changed by massive waves of immigration. It will take many generations to distill a national culture. Further, in our current era of globalization, the events leading to the creation of self-centered national cultures in the nineteenth and twentieth centuries are unlikely to repeat themselves. Multiculturalism will continue to characterize Israeli society. The consolidation of the State of Israel will mean recognizing that a diasporic people makes for a "nation of nations" and that the Arab minority is demographically and culturally an important part of Israeli society.

The future of Judaism in Israel will depend in large part on the capacity to separate religion from the state. Though the ultra-Orthodox rabbinate controls parts of the civil justice system (weddings, divorce, and public cemeteries) and has the authority to decide who is Jewish for the issuance of identity papers, it does not control who can immigrate to Israel. That decision is left to the Israeli Supreme Court, which has ruled that anyone with a grandparent of Jewish origin can immigrate. In this way, if the children of Theodor Herzl—considered "the father of the nation"—had immigrated to Israel, they would not be considered Jewish by the rabbinic courts, since Herzl's mother-in-law was not Jewish. Nevertheless, in Israel, the rulings of other Jewish denominations, which represent the majority of American Jews, are not recognized as legitimate by the state.

The deepest cultural roots of the Orthodox influence in Israel must be sought in the culture of the pioneers who created the State of Israel. Mostly from Eastern Europe, they reacted against Orthodox culture and made a radical break with it—as opposed to German and U.S. Jews, who reworked and modernized the practice of religious Judaism. For them, Judaism was synonymous with Orthodoxy.

Ultra-Orthodox privileges date back to decisions made by the first Israeli governments, which decided to honor the tradition of Talmudic studies, destroyed by the Holocaust, by exempting a small group of students from military service. In the beginning, this privilege was given to a few hundred, but it now includes tens of thousands. By participating in the partisan coalitions that govern the country, religious parties secure entitlements for their constituents. Other groups of ultra-Orthodox Jews living in Israel, mostly Hasidim, do not participate in the government and do not recognize the State of Israel because, ideologically, no Jewish state can exist without the coming of the Messiah.

While still in Europe, a small group of Orthodox Jews who did identify with Zionism created the Mizrahi Party. This party was originally aligned with the Labor Party, but in the past decades it has taken increasingly ultra-nationalist positions.

Most ultra-Orthodox, however, opposed Zionism and the creation of the State of Israel. After independence, Agudath Israel, an umbrella Orthodox organization founded in Europe, created its own political faction that became a part of governing Israeli coalitions. They have pressed for privileges (including exemption from military service) as well as the imposition of religious law on the entire population.

Initially justified on national security grounds, the occupation has acquired legitimacy, for a growing number of sectors within Israeli society, as an expression of "biblical rights." The occupation itself has led to the rebirth of political activism within Orthodox groups, something that had been dormant for two thousand years. A great many settlers and their leaders are associated with Orthodox and ultra-Orthodox religious groups, which claim biblical rights to the occupied territories, thus transforming a nationalist conflict into a religious one.

Some settlers use physical violence against the Palestinian population, and in Israeli cities some ultra-Orthodox organize gangs that harass people who do not follow their view of the Sabbath. Several rabbis have questioned decisions made by legitimate state authorities and given orders authorizing soldiers to disobey their superiors.

The vast majority of modern Israeli Orthodox Jews belong to the nationalist camp. They influence Israeli politics because most of them strongly oppose relinquishing the occupied Palestinian territories. Yet there are important groups of liberal Orthodox, Conservative, Reform, and post-denominational Jews in Israel, including Rabbis for Human Rights, who are opponents of the occupation and proponents of a pluralistic vision of Judaism.

Jewish fundamentalism has acquired the dimensions of a political project, representing a systematic effort among sectors of the Orthodox rabbinate to recover the hegemony that they lost with the advent of modernity. When taken word for word, the Talmud is extremely authoritarian, and its punishments are violent. If they were never applied in practice, it was because Talmudic Judaism never had a state behind it.

The growth of religious power and the weakening of the pioneers' new version of Judaism confront Israeli society with the problem of creating a new secular culture. It was an illusion to think that it would be sufficient to reunite the Jews in one location from which a new Jewish culture would naturally be created. This illusion reinforces the passivity of many secular Israelis who believe that living in Israel ensures a Jewish life.

Many secular Israelis work for the advancement of secular Jewish culture, but most of them still passively accept Orthodox and ultra-Orthodox impositions. Rather than having to answer the basic existential and cultural questions — What constitutes Jewish Israeli culture? What is the role of religion? Who is a Jew? What is a Jewish education? — they allow the Orthodox to define the parameters against which they rebel. They would do better to advance their own definition of the meaning of Judaism in a secular, democratic Jewish state. A national culture is always the product of citizens' demands and the mobilization of human resources and public policy.

Although they identify with the fate of Israel, most Jews wish to remain in the Diaspora, enjoying social integration in their national societies and global culture. Zionism still struggles to recognize this fact. Life in the Diaspora continues to be seen negatively, as leading to the abandonment of Judaism through "assimilation."

Zionism proved to be right in certain respects and wrong in others; as with every political ideology, it focused excessively on certain themes and ignored others. It erred profoundly by underestimating the importance of the Diaspora to the survival of Judaism and Israel. An ideology that compares Israel's capacity for self-defense with the defenselessness of Jews in the Diaspora makes a false comparison. The existence of the State of Israel continues to be fundamental for persecuted Jews, and it strengthens the dignity of diasporic Jews and their willingness to defend themselves. Whether for a small state like Israel or a community in the Diaspora, it is always necessary to count on external support, and the State of Israel itself has had fundamental support from both the Diaspora and allied countries.

The State of Israel has left profound marks on contemporary Jewish identity. It has radically changed the Jewish self-image, fostered a rich artistic culture, and created academic centers that generate fruitful intellectual production. The renaissance of Hebrew as a daily language also represents an important contribution. Although for decades there has been a Zionist policy to supplant Yiddish with Hebrew, Yiddish faded away naturally in the New World and was destroyed by the Holocaust and Stalinism in Eastern Europe. Though it has not become as widely used in the Diaspora as Yiddish or Ladino once were, the

Hebrew language has become a source of identity for Jews around the world.

The State of Israel will certainly remain a central reference point for Judaism. But it is not the only reference point, nor should it be. The construction of Jewish identities in the Diaspora requires an affirmation of the variety of ways to live Jewishly. Israeli governments tend to confuse their specific policies with the interests of world Jewry, and community leaders in the Diaspora tend to use their contacts in Israel to magnify their own standing. Both do a disservice to Judaism.

The founders of the State of Israel sought to break with the negative values they associated with the Diaspora: resignation, fear, weakness, submission. Yet in doing so they forgot the principal lesson of Jewish history: institutions that support themselves through military power alone are fleeting because the strength of a culture lies in its values. If it becomes merely a reaction to the Diaspora, Israel will not be able to make peace with the Palestinians and will place its own existence in danger, thereby threatening the communities in the Diaspora as well. The future of Judaism demands a synthesis of Israeli and diasporic values, a synthesis between the readiness to use force when needed and the knowledge that in the long run force does not guarantee the survival of a people.

Postmodernity, Diaspora, and Individualized Judaism

In modernity, Jews faced two challenges: adapting to a new external context and at the same time engaging in dialogue or confrontation with the Judaism of the previous generation. As a consequence, each generation produced its own version of Judaism. This was a source of enrichment, but it made dialogue with the past and the accumulation of experience more difficult.

In order to understand the current generation of Jews, we must analyze the context in which they live, a context profoundly different from that in which Judaism developed during the twentieth century. We live in an era in which history, political ideology, and rationalism—though still culturally important—have lost much of their strength as an inspirational source for collective action. These are times characterized by "the collapse of the future," by disbelief in constant progress. We live in an era when people are increasingly aware that scientific rationality does not possess the answers to all questions and when subjective, individual problems increasingly take people away from activism in politics and public issues. In short, these are times that have eroded the responses of mid-twentieth-century Judaism.

The postmodern world, ever more global and unified through mass communication and mass consumption, creates individuals who participate in multiple "tribal" subcultures and networks that are constantly mutating—but in which they feel uprooted and alone. For those who are unable to live with uncertainty, with the loss of fixed collective meaning and the decomposition of traditional values, religion becomes a safe harbor.

Cultural globalization and homogenization, the emptying of public life, the questioning of reason and universal values, the substitution of individualism and the search for personal happiness in place of collective utopias—these are the new sociocultural substrata from which contemporary Judaism must generate new, creative answers.

For the past two thousand years, the Jewish condition has been lived in coexistence with many aspects of contemporary culture. The Jew, uprooted, had the world as a reference point and uncertainty as a parameter. As a cosmopolitan, he was a natural navigator between cultures. In this sense, Judaism and postmodernity have strong affinities.

In a way, postmodernity has "naturalized" the Jewish condition. In modernity, Jews were forced into a double subjectivity. In public they were made to demonstrate their integration into the national culture, while in private they maintained their sense of faithfulness to Judaism. In postmodernity this schizophrenia is no longer necessary. Today, having multiple identities and loyalties is the norm. Increasingly, these identities have sub- and supra-national reference points. The Diaspora, which had previously appeared to be an anomaly, is now becoming a universal phenomenon. Ethnic or gender identities and ideologies such as the discourse on human rights or environmentalism have decentralized the place of national identity in contemporary democracies. Abandonment of ethnic particularism in the name of creating a new universal society is no longer the order of the day.

The ideologies that had substituted tradition as the key to interpreting the meaning of personal experience are now gone. Judging what is right or wrong has become a personal decision made without external authority to support one's choice. Each reading of a text is now a personal effort to understand its meaning. Spinoza's dream of recovering the literal meaning of the biblical text no longer makes sense because postmodern philosophy has shown that every reading is an interpretation. By definition, every *pshat* is a *drash*, and what we think of as the literal or original meaning of a text is itself a new, personal interpretation.

The young Jew of today is far removed from the modern Jew who was tortured by questions such as *What does it mean to be a Jew? What is Jewish identity?* Behind these questions was the necessity of making a choice between particularism and universalism, national solidarity and ethnic community, group tradition and world utopia. It is now no longer necessary to choose.

In a world that has increasingly ceased to treat Judaism as an aberration and the Jew as a misfit incapable of adaptation, Judaism should be able to flourish. Cosmopolitanism, the capacity to coexist with diverse cultures, has become a virtue and is even the subject of academic courses. The end of "total" ideologies, with their exclusion of anything that did not fit the discourse, is without doubt a healthy development.

But the historical dynamic is paradoxical: while different types of diasporas are now flourishing around the world, Judaism has become "de-diasporized." Eighty percent of Jews are located in Israel and the United States, and most of them do not experience Judaism as a diasporic condition.

Modern Hebrew has two words for diaspora: *galut* (exile) and *tefutsoth* (diaspora). The first has a strong negative connotation, that of an external imposition, the fate of living as an oppressed minority in a strange land. The second is neutral, referring simply to a group dispersed to foreign lands. The experience of Jews in the world today is characterized by diaspora with a small *d*, not exile. It demands that we create new narratives of Jewish history, different from the ones that sustain traditional religious Orthodoxy and Zionism — narratives that value the Diaspora as a source of richness and creativity, as integral to the survival of the Jewish people.

These new narratives must increasingly develop a Jewish identity that does not have, at its core, histories of persecution and victimization. Jewish identity is becoming an expression of positive choice, an ethnic identity rather than a stigmatized one. It is more and more about liberty, less about destiny. The positive assessment of transnational identities and globalization and the social success of the Jewish

Diaspora put the relations between the State of Israel and the Diaspora into a new perspective. Zionism's dream of normalizing the Jewish people seems to have been inversely accomplished in the postmodern world. The diasporic condition has become the norm, and nationalism, though still alive, is a normative framework in crisis. The world has become more Jewish, and Jews have been "normalized" because of the new cosmopolitan values associated with the global media and the international circulation of people.

The recognition of the legitimacy of the Diaspora and the diasporic condition does not imply dismissing the role of the State of Israel. The national state has been weakened as a cultural value but continues to be relevant. What should change is the relationship between the Diaspora and the State of Israel. In addition, it should be recognized that each diasporic national community is unique.

Judaism is a successful synthesis of local and global, particular and universal. From its stigmatized identity, in some measure still present in parts of Europe, it was transformed into a valued ethnic identity, particularly in the United States and most Latin American countries. In many communities, mixed marriages are increasingly perceived by non-Jews as a positive step toward integration into the local society. And after almost two thousand years, there are non-Jews who are increasingly choosing to become Jewish via conversion. Within Judaism, postdenominational movements seek to incorporate feminism, environmentalism, and general political activism in order to bring tradition up to date. Esoteric and mystical traditions like the Kabbalah have been repackaged as self-help manuals and have been transformed into extremely successful "exports" for non-Jews, publicly embraced by celebrities. Denominations from across the spectrum, from the Reform to the Lubavitch, are retooling their message into self-help formulas.

Today, in most cases, Judaism has stopped being a constant presence in the daily lives of most Jews. Postmodern Judaism is an individualized Judaism that people use in accordance with their moods and circumstances. It is an individual construction that emphasizes particular aspects of Judaism. Jews remember Jewish practices and institutions in a sporadic way or in relation to life-cycle events—births and deaths, weddings and *b'nai mitzvoth*, illnesses, the loss of parents or grandparents, existential crises. Judaism has ceased to be a product of institutions that define a whole lifestyle, one in which the community prevails over the individual; it has been transformed into a two-way street, because in order for institutions to survive, they must offer services that adapt to the demands of individuals who use their services in a personalized way.

The Diaspora, previously an anomaly in societies based on the national state, has become a widespread paradigm for collective identity building. Instead of being a closed space, Judaism has become a personal construction, a cultural bricolage in which each individual appropriates the products of Jewish culture in his or her own way.

A flexible Jewish identity is not something negative, but a monolithic identity imposed on an individual certainly is. It is like a straightjacket or a bunker where a person hides because he or she cannot bear the freedom of choice or the diversity of cultural experience that the contemporary world has to offer.

A Jewish identity lived openly permits flexibility in choosing from the diversity of Jewish cultural offerings. This leads to an expansion of the consumer market for "Jewish goods" and Jewish identity in an expanding marketplace no longer tied solely to close-knit groups.

If in modernity Judaism challenged the individual to leave aside his or her personal interests and help change the world, in postmodernity it is the individual who challenges Judaism to find the answers to his or her subjective problems and give meaning to his or her place in society. Obviously, in today's dominant, solipsistic culture, in this "Me" generation, the danger lies in transforming Judaism into another prop for the narcissistic culture of our era.

National Judaisms

The emphasis on a negative view of the Diaspora fostered the conviction that Jews and Judaism had been held hostage in inhospitable places—way stations along the path to the Messiah or the State of Israel. This produced a profoundly distorted view of Jewish history. Judaism has developed and been enriched thanks to its capacity to coexist, interact with, enjoy, absorb, contribute to, and generate new forms of cultural synthesis. Whether in cuisine, music, art, knowledge, language, or forms of religiosity and belief, Judaism has always been rooted in different cultures and places.

A perfect example of this is the culture of the Spanish Jews, the Sephardim. The Sephardim continued the use of Ladino for five centuries after their expulsion from the Iberian Peninsula! What better expression of syncretism than the use, even today, of the hamsa, an amulet in the shape of a hand with Hebrew inscriptions? Its origins lie in the legend of Fatima Zahra, daughter of the Prophet Muhammad. Although Jews consider Hebrew their sacred language, Aramaic, the *lingua franca* of the Middle East for many centuries before and after Jesus, is used in the Talmud, the liturgy, the Pentateuch (*Targum Onkeles*—the Onkeles translation), and religious rites. For example, the *Kaddish* (memorial prayer for the dead) and *Kol Nidre* (said at the beginning of the evening service on Yom Kippur, the Day of Atonement, the most sacred day of the year) are recited in Aramaic.

Different local contexts generate great diversity and at times great intercommunal conflict. During the French Revolution, for example,

Sephardic Jews sought to distinguish themselves from Ashkenazi Jews by demanding citizenship, arguing that they did not share the "backwardness" of the Alsace-Lorraine communities. Nobel Prize-winning writer Elias Canetti recalls in his memoirs that in Bulgaria a Sephardic marriage to an Ashkenazi Jew was taboo.

I myself remember from my own childhood the difficulty of understanding how someone could be considered Jewish and not speak Yiddish! Prejudice and mistrust between the Orthodox Sephardic and Ashkenazi worlds, and within their different regions, was intense. When they arrived in the New World, these communities organized themselves according to their region of origin. The best way for someone to discover the diversity, tensions, and differences among the various strains of Judaism, as rooted in different local histories, is to visit today's Israel.

Many Jewish community leaders find it difficult to acknowledge the profound integration between Jewish culture and the local cultures in which they are rooted. For some, the Jew must forever remain "the other," a body estranged from the national culture. The fear of "assimilation" comes from the cultural interpenetration fostered by contemporary society, which dissolves cultural borders.

And yet Judaism has survived since biblical times because of its capacity to adapt to the most diverse cultures. It was thanks to his assimilation into European culture that Theodor Herzl, a secular Jew, created political Zionism.

What is the definition of an assimilated Jew? Diverse currents of Judaism have decried assimilation in order to disqualify and demonize those who choose not to be affiliated with any of them. But history teaches us that no single Jewish denomination or intellectual or social movement can exhaust all possibilities; each innovation represents a contribution that renews and strengthens Judaism, just as Hasidism and Zionism did in their time.

In the demonology constructed around assimilation, German Judaism holds a place of distinction. Never in Jewish history—and perhaps even in universal history—did a relatively small group make such an important contribution to art, science, culture, religion, and civilization.

But the Nazi tragedy made German Jews into scapegoats for those who promoted a paranoid version of history. German Jews would have been fools, if not frankly traitors, to have believed in the value of German culture. In precise historical circumstances, a fanatical and criminal regime took power, but that never disqualified the contributions of German Jews, without which neither Judaism nor humanity would be what it is today.

If there is a lesson to learn from the experience of German Judaism, it is not that Jews should avoid integrating into the local culture; it is that they should always be aware of the destructive nature of the modern state when it falls into the hands of authoritarian regimes. Modern society, in its capitalist or communist versions, has shown that the values of equality, liberty, and fraternity can rapidly be denied by political forces capable of mobilizing xenophobic sentiments. The enemy of minorities is not local culture but authoritarian regimes. Those who defend a vision of a homogeneous national culture simply develop an instrument of power to exclude all those who dissent.

Judaism as Endurance, Cognitive Dissonance, and Collective Guilt

None of the psychological characteristics attributed to Jews are monopolized by them, and fewer still are equally distributed among individuals. It is natural to be proud of being part of a group that produced Einstein and Freud, but standing in the shadow of great figures does not make one equal to them. It can provide an incentive for an individual to improve him or herself, provided it does not transform a child into the victim of a Jewish mother who expects that someday he (rather than she . . .) will receive the Nobel Prize!

The characteristics identified as being part of "Jewish psychology" are present in individuals of all cultures. At the same time, though not possessing a monopoly on any human characteristic, many Jews do possess certain traits and skills that are a product of their history and that have favored their success in modern circumstances. These characteristics are present even among Jews who do not define themselves as such, because they are products of a long historical and collective experience.

As mentioned earlier, Jews survived persecutions throughout the Middle Ages by maintaining a culture of their own and a particularly high level of literacy. Belief in messianic redemption and in being God's chosen people, as well as strong family values and solid institutions of mutual support, assured cohesion and social control. This empowered Jews both as a group and as individuals by creating an enormous capacity for spiritual resistance, the ability to endure adverse situations and develop creative strategies for survival.

Although Jews were an oppressed group, they were able to maintain an extremely positive self-image. Freud explains this positive self-image as a compensatory mechanism for the blows the Jews have suffered at the hands of other nations since biblical times. But not every neurotic becomes Leonardo da Vinci, nor does every small, defeated people survive and create a positive self-image in the way the Jews have. Whereas oppressed groups tend to internalize their menial position and accept their place in the social hierarchy, Jews managed to maintain high levels of self-confidence and protect themselves from the dominant code that humiliated and excluded them.

This disposition to reject the established rules of the game and refuse to submit to the social order and preestablished hierarchies is referred to as chutzpah (gall, impertinence, insolence, audacity). Chutzpah was particularly effective for another factor, a product of living conditions in the Diaspora—namely, the capacity to cope with cognitive dissonance.

We know that people's general tendency is to align with the opinions of the majority. For centuries, Jews were trained to live in two worlds, the dominant culture on the one hand and their own culture on the other. This training entailed learning to live between two cultures, understanding that there were other ways of being, and, above all, maintaining a worldview that was different from the dominant one. Being a person in the minority demands a constant effort to discern the intentions of the other, to think of oneself while taking the other into consideration.

One of the basic conditions of creativity is the capacity to withstand cognitive dissonance. A creative person is someone who thinks differently, who seeks out his or her own path, who endures and enjoys being a "cognitive dissonant." To think or act differently, to produce innovative ideas and practical solutions, demands a propensity for unconventional, independent thinking, a disposition to follow one's own path and leave aside common sense. Common sense—that is, the code that defines the behavior of the majority of the population—was beyond the reach of Jews.

In Talmudic culture, the capacity for cognitive dissonance served primarily as a strategy for maintaining Judaism in the face of a dominant religion. By the end of the Middle Ages, however,

Jews had begun to express their creativity in commerce, cartography, and navigation. In modern times, freed from external and internal limitations, Jewish creativity expanded to all areas, from science to the arts.

Jewish humor is a particular expression of the reflective nature of the Jewish condition. In order to make bearable the weight of a neurotic relationship with the world, Jewish humor mocks all that is normally taken seriously. It expresses a permanent need to decipher the conduct of the other in order to adapt to external expectations — as in the tragicomedy of a Jewish mother's obsession with the success of her children, the complexity of relations with the non-Jewish world, or the use of convoluted means to obtain a desired result.

Cultural capital, endurance in the face of adversity, chutzpah, the creative capacity produced by being trained to live with cognitive dissonance — all of these enabled Jews to occupy a high percentage of distinguished positions in modern societies. The fight for social ascent and success is also typical of a group that feels profoundly insecure about its future and place in society.

However, the benefits of this success were accompanied by enormous costs. Endurance, chutzpah, and success are characteristics that evoke feelings in others, especially when generated by a minority group. Every story of success, whether collective or individual, leads to the projection of a positive or negative image, to feelings of destructive envy or admiration — but rarely to neutrality.

Jews also have strong feelings of collective guilt (again, this is a generalization based on characteristics that differ from individual to individual). Jews need to overcome the tendency to see themselves through the eyes of non-Jews. Every oppressed group feels guilty for possessing characteristics that are identified as negative by the dominant culture (skin color, gender, sexual orientation). They bear their lot by internalizing, to a greater or lesser degree, the opinions of the oppressor.

In modernity, Jews manifested this tendency vis-à-vis the constant need to justify their right to exist; this continually led them to recall the contribution that Jews have made to humanity, to view themselves as the privileged heirs of a universal ethical discourse born of past suffering. These responses are understandable, but the right to exist does not need to be justified, and a universalist ethic that represses or hides the interests of its proponents ends in self-delusion.

The modern Jewish condition also generated social dissonance. In the twentieth century, the social ascent of Jews did not bring an end to stigma and prejudice; many Jews who were able to rise socially still felt oppressed and marginalized. The promises of the Enlightenment did not seem to materialize within liberal capitalist societies, at least not until the middle of the last century. A further step toward the fulfillment of Enlightenment ideals was needed. Linked to cognitive dissonance, social stigma led a large percentage of Jews to identify with the oppressed and become activists in support of revolutionary political causes. The old messianic dream became grafted onto secular utopias, and Jewish intellectuals were disproportionately represented in these political movements.

In recent decades, this scene has changed profoundly. Revolutionary utopias have lost their momentum, and the demands of oppressed groups have fragmented into corporate demands, with each victim seeking recognition for his or her own specific grievances. In most countries, in turn, Jews have consolidated their possession of middle-class social positions, and in good economic times, anti-Jewish attitudes and discrimination decrease dramatically. However, during times of economic decline, discrimination rises.

As a result of these internal and external transformations, secular Jewish utopianism lost its central role in contemporary secular Judaism. And in fact, the end of political utopias that promote radical new beginnings through forcible social engineering is a salutary development. At the same time, this does not mean that the search for a better world should be abandoned by humanistic Judaism. Instead of omnipotent dreams of revolutionary change, the search for a better society is accomplished via piecemeal projects carried out through practical actions in support of the needy, oppressed, and persecuted, actions born of the personal satisfaction of doing good — without the guarantee of final success offered by religious or political ideologies.

PART THREE

CHALLENGES FACING JUDAISM

Who Speaks for the Jews: Rabbis? Plutocrats? The Israeli Government?

Modern Judaism was created when a new leadership questioned the monopoly held by Orthodox rabbis on the definition of Judaism. This revolution occurred even within the religious establishment. Liberal and then Conservative rabbis affirmed that Orthodox rabbis were not the only source of authority to define the parameters of the Jewish religion. Since the nineteenth century, new intellectual elites, most of them secular, have renewed Judaism and transformed Orthodoxy into a minority current.

The Hebrew language was revivified and modernized by secular Zionist Jews who used it as a daily language, whereas the archaic version known as *Loshon Kodesh* ("The Holy Tongue") was restricted to study and prayer. Yiddish literature and, later, theater and cinema were mostly the work of secular Jewish writers who came from Orthodox life. Yiddish culture, the socialist Bund movement,

Zionism, and the creation of the State of Israel were all led by secular Jews — Leo Pinsker, Theodor Herzl, David Ben-Gurion, Zev Jabotinsky, Moshe Dayan, and Golda Meir, to mention only a few.

In the last few decades, rabbis of all persuasions have regained position in Jewish life. Though it is really not the case, most Jews feel that a rabbi's presence is required at circumcisions, *b'nai mitzvoth*, weddings, and even burials. In the public sphere, some rabbis have become spokespeople for different political and religious positions espoused by their constituents and/or followers.

How was this apparent return to the past possible, especially when it was not supported by traditional structures? In Talmudic Judaism, in contrast to the role of priests in Catholicism, rabbis do not possess special status. In Judaism, no intermediary exists in the relationship between God and man. No Jewish ceremony requires the presence of a rabbi. Circumcision, *b'nai mitzvoth*, weddings, burials, prayers at the synagogue — or any other rite — can be performed without a rabbi. The only requirement, in certain religious ceremonies, is a *minyan*, a presence quorum of ten Jews, who symbolize a community. Though traditionally male, today women are counted in *minyanim* in non-Orthodox denominations.

The Orthodox synagogue my family attended never had a rabbi. Similarly, there were no rabbis at other neighborhood synagogues, nor were there necessarily rabbis at Orthodox Jewish circumcisions, weddings, and burials. Judaism without the presence of a rabbi seemed normal in our community. How did the widespread perception that it is necessary for a rabbi to preside over life-cycle events begin to permeate Jewish communities? Why do people assume that a book about Judaism must be written by a rabbi? Where does the contemporary authority and legitimacy of rabbis come from?

It may come from the convergence of factors whose importance varies from country to country:

1. The professionalization of the rabbinate is relatively recent. The great rabbis who contributed to the Talmud earned their bread in other professions. According to the Talmud, Hillel cut wood; Shammai was a builder; Joshua, a blacksmith; Abba Hoshaya of Turya, a wool washer; Hanina and Oshaya, shoemakers; Karna, a winemaker; Huna, a waterbearer; Abba ben Zemina, a tailor; and so on. A rabbi was not a professional, but a person of wisdom recognized as such by the community. It was only during the Low Middle Ages, around the twelfth century, that the figure of the rabbi as we know it began to emerge. His primary function was to pass judgment in civil matters and make *halakhic* decisions.

2. Reform and Conservative Judaism created a different type of "expert," a professional rabbi possessing modern academic training, a model influenced by nineteenth-century German Protestantism. With cultural drift taking place in many

communities, the modern rabbi was no longer needed as a civic arbiter; conflicts were judged in local secular courts and issues of *Kashrut* lost their relevance. Professional rabbis were maintained by communities whose relationship to Judaism was less intense; a rabbi was someone who would be there to offer sermons and make sure that rituals were performed properly, along with providing personal counseling.

3. What was originally a phenomenon restricted to Reform Judaism became widespread in different types of Jewish communities. While earlier generations of secular Jews had had religious training, against which they rebelled, many among the new generations of secular Jews did not have any notion of what Jewish tradition was. Naturally they delegated this knowledge to specialists, including Orthodox rabbis, even if they were not Orthodox themselves. This is normally the case when performing rituals, in imitation of the surrounding Christian environment.

The contemporary rabbi is a professional who serves a community. He or she certainly contributes to the upkeep of Judaism, and many rabbis make important contributions to its renewal. But they do not possess any monopoly over Judaism nor are they its spokespeople.

During the Middle Ages and at the beginning of modern times, there was a division of labor between rabbis and wealthier Jews. The rabbis acted as leaders of the Jewish community and were intermediaries with local ruling powers.

There was (and to some extent still is) a tradition whereby rich Jews would marry their daughters and their dowries off to the best rabbis in town, thus ensuring the sustenance of the rabbi's family. This model was repeated in each generation: while the men studied, the women took care of family and business affairs.

Rich and poor have always lived together in Jewish communities. It was only at the turn of the twentieth century in Eastern Europe and the United States that working Jews and intellectuals came to identify with ideologies in which class struggle played a central role. Yet Judaism's social diversity has always been a factor in its survival. Rich Jews constructed synagogues, acted as philanthropists, and supported Yiddish culture, the Zionist movement, and the construction of the State of Israel—even though for a long time the Zionist movement was dominated by socialist tendencies. Despite the tensions that the social differences of wealth and the power associated with it can create, social diversity is generally an enriching phenomenon that is often expressed in solidarity and support for community institutions—something that should be applauded. However, because of the relative scarcity of humanistic and secular institutions in both Israel and the Diaspora, most Jewish philanthropic resources are channeled through religious denominations. This results in a vicious circle in which a major portion of Jews are not reached.

Finally, the government of the State of Israel tends to claim that it represents the Jewish people as a whole, but this is obviously not the case. Demographics play a huge role in the maintenance of Israeli security, so one of the state's main policies is aimed at encouraging Jewish immigration and garnering support for its foreign policy in the Diaspora. These are both legitimate interests, but we should not confuse the political interests and viewpoint of Israeli governments with those of the Jewish people in the Diaspora.

Secular intellectuals, particularly writers, artists, and scientists, continue to play an important role in all forms of Judaism, in both the Diaspora and Israel. They serve as cultural ambassadors and are the loudest moral voices of Judaism to the outside world.

The intellectual orphanhood of many Jewish institutions is dramatized by the many Jewish intellectuals who have abandoned community life. The challenge for secular Jews is to reclaim the role played by intellectuals and secular leaders during the last two centuries. In some cases, creating new leadership might include promoting the image of the secular, humanistic rabbi, a practice that is advancing in the United States and Israel.

A secular, humanistic rabbi is a person who acts as a community leader and performs ceremonies because of his or her knowledge and vocation. Indeed, this is the deepest tradition associated with the figure of the rabbi, a person to whom the community delegates certain functions and a teacher who is not endowed with any particular power.

Who is Jewish? Weddings and Burials

In the Orthodox Talmudic tradition, when a son or daughter married a non-Jew, the parents were supposed to treat them not as if they had died (for that would require mourning) but as if they had never existed; their names and memory were to be erased or, as we would say today, deleted. Today, when the child of an Orthodox Jew marries out, the parents observe the seven days of mourning and cut the child out of their lives.

The definition of who is Jewish is one of the inheritances of Talmudic culture that faces modern Judaism and demands to be openly confronted. Every social group has entrance criteria. Matrilineal descent is one, but it is too limiting because it excludes the children of men who have married out. Instituted in the post-biblical period and born of a particular historical context, this rule has become obsolete. The matrilineal rule errs on the side of excess because it continues to define as a Jew someone who has a Jewish mother but has opted not to identify with Judaism — even when that person has converted to another religion. Imposing Jewish identity in this way was justifiable during times of forced conversion, but not today. For example, Sir Nicholas George Winton, who saved 669 Jewish children from the Holocaust, was denied the Israeli title of "Righteous Gentile" by Yad Vashem, Israel's Holocaust Martyrs' and Heroes' Remembrance Authority, because he was considered to be Jewish, despite the fact that his parents converted to Christianity and he had been raised in the Christian tradition.

It also errs by omission because it excludes those — generally children of a marriage in which the father is Jewish — who want to be Jews but do not wish to submit themselves to conversion. This has no biblical legitimacy. Indeed, if the principle of matrilineage were strictly applied, there would be no Jews. Abraham, Isaac, Jacob, Moses, David, and Solomon were all married to non-Jewish women, and the Bible makes no mention of their conversion.

The priestly line (Cohain and Levi) continues to be determined by patrilineal descent. It has been a role passed from father to son without interruption throughout Jewish history. In the Bible, when Moses is criticized by his brother Aaron and sister Miriam for marrying a non-Jew (*Kushit*, of African origin), God punishes Miriam by infecting her with leprosy. When the Bible does express a preoccupation with mixed marriage, it is in the context of the later books (Leviticus and Deuteronomy), and the concern is that non-Jewish women will introduce idolatrous practices.

One explanation for the adoption of matrilineage is that maternity, unlike paternity, can be verified. Another explanation is that it was a form of protecting mothers who gave birth after being raped by conquering soldiers, particularly during the Roman period.

Patrilineage continues to be a common practice in the Diaspora. Recent genetic research indicates that a great number of Jewish communities in the Diaspora have patrilineal origins, the result of weddings between Jews and local women. In short, matrilineage alone is not supported by either biblical or historical sources. It is a convention that came to predominate during a particular historical period of Judaism.

In the modern era there was initially greater tolerance toward mixed marriages among the rich and famous. No one dared criticize the Rothschilds for marrying non-Jews, and Jews are proud of individuals like Albert Einstein and other Nobel Prize winners and famous artists, all married to non-Jews. Einstein was even invited to be the second president of Israel, which, had he accepted, would have meant Israel would have had a non-Jewish first lady. The most popular Chanukah song in the United States, "The Chanukah Song," from Adam Sandler's album *Eight Crazy Nights*, puts it this way: "Paul Newman's half Jewish; Goldie Hawn's half too. Put them together — what a fine lookin' Jew!" and, "Harrison Ford's a quarter Jewish — not too shabby!"

Jews are no longer surrounded by pagan peoples, Jewish women are no longer subject to mass violation, and paternity is now verifiable. The real danger today is that the children of mixed marriages will be marginalized by the prejudices found in certain Jewish communities.

The majority of Jews perceive every human life as having equal value and sacredness. We live in a world where people seek to prioritize their own well-being and happiness and do not consider differences of origin to be an obstacle to love and coexistence. Naturally, social interaction leads to a greater number of mixed marriages. Around half of the Jews in the Diaspora marry non-Jews, and their parents find themselves divided between maintaining their attachment to the past or accepting new rules that will not exclude their children from Judaism. Certainly, very few among them are predisposed to "deleting" a son or a daughter, and it is rare even among modern Orthodox Jews to find people who mourn their children as if they had died. Traditional institutions that define "who is a Jew" are slowly adapting to this new reality.

In Israel, the continued Orthodox monopoly on the definition of who is Jewish leads to a paradox: Orthodox Jewish tradition is matrilineal whereas Muslim tradition is patrilineal; according to Israeli law (which gives equal recognition to the authority of Muslim clerics) the offspring of a Muslim and a Jew would be condemned to remain simultaneously in both religions. In recent years, there have been proposals to break the rabbinate's monopoly on conversions through the creation of a rite of "secular conversion" that would allow those who are not religious to be integrated into Jewish life.

A common sad scenario in Israel involves young soldiers from the former Soviet Union who die on the battlefront. In the course of burial preparations, the Orthodox rabbi declares that the soldier is not Jewish since his mother had not converted to Judaism according to Orthodox law administered by specific rabbis (hundreds of thousands of immigrants from the former Soviet Unions are Jews by patrilineage). Therefore, the boy's burial in the military cemetery, or any other cemetery controlled by the rabbinate, is prohibited. In some cases, the soldier's body is "repatriated" to his country of origin (or that of his parents); in other cases, the body is buried in a "private" cemetery, generally on a kibbutz that maintains cemeteries not under the jurisdiction of the rabbinate.

In several countries in the Diaspora, there are numerous kinds of Jewish cemeteries; in certain cases, cemeteries are administrated like condominiums by the various religious denominations, and in some countries, burials remain in the hands of the Orthodox rabbis who are often insensitive or unyielding to the family ties of the deceased.

Secular humanistic Judaism, Reform Judaism, and some rabbis in the Reconstructionist and Renewal movements accept the child of either a Jewish mother or father as Jewish as long as he or she is educated within Judaism, has completed the rites of passage (circumcision, bar/bat mitzvoth) and defines him or herself as Jewish. On the other hand, for Jews who have converted to other religions, conversion is required if they want to return to Judaism. The Conservative movement, although divided, still maintains the matrilineal principle.

North American Conservative and Reform Judaism have pressured Israel and demanded that conversions performed by their rabbis in the Diaspora be accepted as legitimate, and they have been successful. At the same time, conversions performed by Conservative and Reform rabbis in Israel are still not accepted.

In the Diaspora, too, conversions performed by Reform rabbis are questioned by Conservative rabbis, who find themselves questioned by Orthodox rabbis — and even more so by the ultra-Orthodox. In the same way, many of the conversions performed by the Orthodox are questioned by the ultra-Orthodox, and within Orthodoxy there are divisions over the matter. These divisions are extremely positive because they indicate definitively that Judaism today is pluralistic. What is needed is the institutionalization of de facto pluralism in Jewish communities and in Israel.

Anti-Semitism and the Relations between Yidn and Goyim

Jews in the Diaspora were easily transformed into scapegoats for those who needed someone to blame for the uncertainties of modern life, especially during times of economic, social, and cultural upheaval.

With relatively high percentages of participation in both communist political parties and the world of business, Jews were presented as an invisible power, plotters of conspiracies that drove the world order.

The Jewish inclination toward innovation and social success produced contradictory sentiments. Whether characterized by admiration or hatred, these reactions were rooted in the contradictions of modernity. In a world with egalitarian values, Jews stand out because, in societies that are individualistic, they have a strong sense of solidarity. They are innovative, and yet they somehow manage to maintain their traditions. At the same time, Jewish success perpetuated or revived old prejudices produced by Christianity and Islam.

Jews are valued by people, ideologies, and cultures that are oriented toward the future; however, for those who romanticize the past, the Jew tends to be represented as the destroyer of an idealized world. The association of the State of Israel with the United States, for example, has produced an unlikely alliance between Islamic fundamentalists and antiglobalization activists.

Centuries of persecution have transformed anti-Semitism into the yardstick that yidn (the term for Jews in Yiddish) still use, mainly unconsciously, to measure their relationships with goyim (the term for non-Jews in the Talmud; in the Bible, however, goyim refers generically to all peoples, including the Jews).

This reading of non-Jewish behavior is understandable for a group that experienced humiliation and persecution for centuries and then suffered the enormous trauma of the Holocaust. The Jewish condition is characterized by a feeling of fragility that is difficult to convey in the contemporary world, a world in which so many people experience need, suffering, and oppression. Although the Jews were victims for many long centuries, most of them have now spent decades living in prosperity, even though there are still many more Jews living in poverty than the popular imagination would like to admit.

Yet many non-Jews do not understand why Jews present themselves as victims when they are relatively well-off socially; for Jews, conversely, the nonexistence of persecution in the majority of countries where they now live does not eliminate the fear that anti-Semitism could reappear. This fear is not irrational, especially because there is always the possibility of a resurgence of political discourse that transfers the "guilt" for social problems onto an "external" minority group. Political anti-Semitism continues to be a potential danger even in advanced capitalist countries. In many Muslim countries, Jews, Israel, and the United States continue to be vilified and treated like scapegoats for the difficulties experienced in adapting to modernity.

The situation is somewhat similar regarding the difficulty some Israelis have in understanding that a large portion of international public opinion is sympathetic toward the Palestinians. This support is based on the fact that most Palestinians live in conditions of poverty and oppression, whereas Israelis enjoy a higher standard of living and have a strong and sophisticated army. And yet the Israeli perception of being treated unfairly is not self-deception. It is fed by critics of Israeli foreign policy who support groups that advocate the destruction of Israel. These critics confuse the legitimate objective of creating a Palestinian state with ideologies and leaders driven by a genocidal agenda.

The danger of anti-Semitism and the difficulty of communicating the fragility of the Jewish condition have led a majority of community leaders to denounce any form of expression that might have a negative connotation related to Jews or the policies of the governments of the State of Israel. Without a doubt, there is anti-Semitism that should be denounced and fought, yet it is of no help to call any remark critical of Israel anti-Semitic, suggesting that it implies hatred of Jews everywhere.

Each case needs to be judged individually. Unfortunately, racism, sexism, and other forms of discrimination produce an industry of victimization, of leaders and institutions that promote themselves through denunciation, leading to a distorted or exaggerated version of the facts. Each case needs to be carefully thought through, but the hypersensitivity of the oppressed does not justify labeling any politically incorrect form of expression as racial hatred.

Particularly in the public sphere, respect for the feelings of others plays a fundamental role in building a society in which no one feels that his or her human dignity is being negated. The objective is to advance increasing mutual respect while taking into account cultural baggage such as linguistic habits, types of humor, and unconscious prejudice. As Sartre put it, people should not be categorized as racist or anti-racist; they should be categorized according to whether they accommodate or confront the racism that resides in each of us.

An inadvertent comment about race, religion, sex, or ethnicity does not transform a person into a racist, anti-Semite, homophobe, or sexist. The concept of racism itself hides a diversity of situations. A prejudiced comment does not imply that an individual is predisposed to joining the Ku Klux Klan or the Nazi Party or that they are imbued with racial hatred. The majority of people who make such comments excuse themselves when they realize they have caused offense.

Every group has prejudices, negative stereotypes, and jokes about their neighbors and other groups. Of course, groups that associate these prejudices with a history of oppression are more sensitive to them. The tendency to cry "fire" even when there is only the spark of political incorrectness in a comment is typical of many institutions and community leaders who make the denunciation of anti-Semitism their raison d'être and the only subject they can talk about. There is no doubt that real fires do exist, and a concerted effort should be made to fight them. In lesser cases, however, Jewish institutions should act pedagogically.

To a greater or lesser degree, anti-*goy*ism or *goy*phobia exists among many Jews, generated and reinforced by the long history of Jewish persecution. The view that anti-Judaism led to massacres and that anti-*goy*ism is innocuous still does not justify its acceptance. Contemporary humanistic Judaism should accept the task of self-analysis and self-transformation in its relationship to *goyim*. Comments with negative connotations about *goyim* are relatively common in conversation among Jews. Does this imply hatred, denial of the humanity of others, or destructive intent? Certainly not. Nevertheless, it remains true that focusing on the reality of anti-Semitism has allowed institutionalized Judaism and most Jewish intellectuals to avoid the problematic dimensions that many Jews manifest in their relations with non-Jews.

To be clear, this is not to explain anti-Semitism in terms of Jewish characteristics. Hatred feeds on itself, not on the characteristics of others. Nor is it to deny the importance of fighting anti-Semitism. What is needed is the recognition of characteristics within Judaism that must be changed. This should be done not to please others but to enable Judaism to fully reflect humanistic values. To paraphrase Sartre, we need to ask not so much whether there is or is not a tendency to devalue the *goy*; rather, we need to ask what we can do to fight this tendency, rooted as it is in two thousand years of history.

Traditional rabbinical Judaism ended up closing the Jewish world in upon itself. In general, the interpretations that separated Jews from non-Jews hewed to the opposition between pure and impure (for some ultra-Orthodox Jews the Sabbath rest can be broken to save *only* a Jewish life). However, the Bible tells us that God created humanity, not only Jews, in his image. It also enshrines the commandment to respect "the stranger who lives among you" and love them because they are like you.

As mentioned previously, according to the Talmud, those who accepted the Noachide laws were considered to be part of the community, and their children were seen as potential Jews. This opening of the Talmud to non-Jews was in great part abandoned due to the prohibitions on proselytizing imposed by Christianity and Islam.

This anti-*goyim* attitude, based in religious tradition, assumed dramatic form during the centuries of persecution in Europe. Until recently, there continued to be a basic sentiment that all *goyim* were potentially anti-Semitic. The relationship between Jew and *goy* included a mixture of fear, distrust, and resentment. In certain cultural contexts this was expressed as contempt for non-Jewish life.

The prejudices that sometimes characterize the Jewish response to *goyim* are a taboo topic in Jewish education. That should change. Even when dealing with the past, dehumanizing *goyim* dehumanizes and weakens Jews as well. When confronted with prejudice, instead of establishing a dialogue, the tendency is to class oneself as a victim, shutting down the conversation. If we understand our own prejudices, we will be better able to build bridges with others and help them change their attitudes.

The Future of Judaism

After the disasters suffered during the first half of the twentieth century, the second half was much more hospitable to both Jews and Judaism. Anti-Semitism as state policy "officially" disappeared, though it still lingers in some parts of Central and Eastern Europe. In general, Jews are members of the middle classes and occupy positions of distinction in diverse social spheres. However, if anything is certain about the future, it is that it is unpredictable, uncontrollable, and subject to change.

The context that permitted the success (and drama) experienced by Jews and Judaism in modern times is changing rapidly. What was this context? Jewish populations were mainly concentrated in Europe and then the United States, regions that have driven the economic, political, cultural, and technological revolutions of the modern world. The Jewish contribution to the development of modern culture is directly associated with the possibilities that modern societies provided for Jews.

Now we are experiencing a shift in the global balance of power; the center of economic and military power is incrementally being transferred to Asia. Europe and the United States will continue to watch their stature dissipate.

More than eighty percent of the world's Jews live in the United States and Israel. The rest are located mostly in Europe. This demographic fact presents various challenges to the future of Jews and Judaism. The gradual loss of stature in the world economic and political order of the United States and Europe and the transfer of the dynamic center of the world economy to Asia will mean that Jews will be increasingly located on the periphery of the international system. The new international order may generate new conflicts of power, sometimes in the guise of intercultural confrontations. The relative marginalization of the West will affect the cultural and political dynamics of currently advanced countries. Certainly, this process will redefine the vision that the West has of itself, as well as the place of Jews and Judaism within it.

For example, the consequences of this change for the State of Israel will be dramatic. Its strategic alliance with the United States, which over the past few decades has assured its security, can be relied upon only as long as the United States itself remains the world's major power. Ultimately, the long-term future of the State of Israel depends on peace and integration in the Middle East.

The central challenge that arises for Judaism is not whether the world will change but how to face these changes. The narrow view — that the only ways to remain Jewish are to live in Israel or become an Orthodox Jew in the Diaspora—still pervades some community institutions. It could be transformed into a self-fulfilling prophecy to the extent that a diagnosis can influence behavior and become reality. On the other hand, if Judaism bets on a pluralistic vision, its chances for success will be much greater. After all, demography counts in the Diaspora as well as in Israel.

The appeal ultra-Orthodoxy holds for those who have not been born into it reflects diverse sociological factors. They are at first attracted to what looks to be exotic and therefore must be "authentic." They do not yet understand that they are looking at a Jew dressed in the style of an eighteenth-century Polish nobleman and that the Yiddish he speaks is a language derived from German.

For many secular Jews the fear of changing the way they practice Judaism sometimes leads them to Orthodox synagogues, despite the fact that Orthodoxy does not reflect their own values. Some secular Jews who are preoccupied with the future of Judaism consider Orthodoxy to be a guarantee of Judaism's continuity, despite disagreeing with it, often vehemently. It could be that Orthodox Judaism offers safe mechanisms for maintaining Judaism, but Orthodoxy itself will not appeal to most Jews who want to participate fully in contemporary society.

Although exclusionary Judaism will always exist, most Jews feel that their Jewish identity should be congenial and express modern values. Judaism has become a culture of individual choices, and this individualization affects even the Orthodox and ultra-Orthodox. There are disciples of Orthodoxy who develop their own personal version of Judaism and who obey certain mitzvoth but not others.

A Judaism that is inclusive and unafraid of proselytism constitutes the only alternative for Judaism's survival. One of the tragedies of the inherited memory of medieval persecutions was the transformation of necessity into a virtue, through which Judaism internalized Catholic and Islamic prohibitions against proselytizing.

The Kabbalah, best marketed worldwide by the Berg family, attracts a wide, non-Jewish public made up of consumers of esoteric products. These consumers exemplify the creation of new cultural spaces on the non-Jewish periphery, spaces that draw them closer to Judaism. For those who espouse secular Judaism, these developments open new possibilities and present new challenges.

The Future of Humanistic and Secular Judaism

Most Jews are humanistic and secular—they define themselves as bearers of a Jewish identity based on personal, historical, and cultural ties, without reference to divine commandments or transcendental beliefs. While "secular" refers to the historical process by which individuals and societies disengaged from the power of religion, humanistic Judaism values individual autonomy and human reason as the basis for validating claims of right and wrong. It affirms the dignity of all human beings and expands our solidarity with and understanding of humanity beyond the limits of our own culture.

In different contexts, Jews may define themselves as humanistic (particularly in the United States), secular (*chilony* in Israel, *laïc* in French), traditionalist, or cultural.

In the contemporary world, what defines the Judaism of humanistic Jews is based mostly on emotions, not on clear and precise narratives. And emotions, by their very nature, are unstable. Whereas modern Judaism, though divided, maintained a great capacity for collective action, secular Jewish life in contemporary society is diffuse and ad hoc, a characteristic that limits the possibility of crystallizing collective action.

At this point in time, the voices of secular Jews as a group are rarely expressed inside the established Jewish leadership around the world, even though they represent a majority of the Jewish people. Most Jewish intellectuals deliberately separate themselves from Jewish institutions of any sort, and most establishment institutions are not interested in giving voice to freethinking Jews, although they like to remember famous Jewish intellectuals—most of them secular humanists.

The main pillars of nonreligious Judaism—socialism and Zionism—have entered into crisis. Both promoted a renewed vision of Jewish history and upheld the values of solidarity and social justice. It is not necessary to comment on the crisis of socialism. As for Zionism, it achieved its dream but has lost much of its appeal in recent decades because of the occupation and its consequences and because it has surrendered to Orthodoxy on many issues.

In the twentieth century, secular Jews were intimately linked to a historical vision of the Jewish people and to the reformulation of messianic hope through the creation of earthly utopias. This was an exercise in substituting socialism for the sacred (represented by the belief in the union between God and the Jewish people), replacing what used to be sacred with the sanctification of the nation or humanity vis-à-vis political projects or universal social ethics.

Today these projects can be judged as both successes and failures. Rooted in the values of secular humanistic Judaism, they succeeded in changing the world. They were successful because they created the State of Israel and had a definite impact on contemporary society—in terms of both social and civil rights. Yet they failed to the extent that the fulfillment of their cultural and social proposals exposed their weaknesses and underscored their particular inattention to the individual—to the subjective dramas and search for individual meaning.

The tripod of modernity—reason, history, and politics—which for generations had confronted and transformed Judaism, entered into crisis. Some looked to Orthodoxy to provide answers and certainties in a world that appeared devoid of meaning. But the majority of the Jewish people did not stop believing in and betting on modernity's great values—that humanity is capable of following the path of freedom and autonomy, greater social justice, peaceful coexistence, and mutual respect between cultures.

In the contemporary world, we have bridges, albeit fragile ones, in place of fusion. These bridges serve to support individuals in finding meaning and connecting with other people. If the individual is the basis for contemporary sociability, he or she exists and can survive thanks only to his or her identification with collective values and social groups.

Individualism creates the illusion that the individual is self-sufficient. This is never the case. The individual needs objects of affection, support, and transcendence. Humanistic Judaism meets all these conditions by offering non-oppressive ways to identify with Jewish tradition and community. The secular humanistic vision allows a person to relate to the past and memories of parents and grandparents without allowing the past to dominate the present. It creates ties to tradition while remaining open to the world. It provides an individual with a sense of solidarity gained through being Jewish within a group that does not lose its sensitivity to the suffering of all human beings.

While maintaining its collective dimension, a renewed humanistic Judaism must address subjective and existential questions. It must include elements of self-help and celebrate its own identity without blind ethnocentrism or narcissistic complacency.

Because memory and history are fundamental to the Jewish people's sense of identity, secular humanists should harmonize them with the new Jewish identity they seek to create. After all, collective memory is always a construction in service of an identity. One way or another, our ideas of the past are nourished by previous versions. But collective memory is always malleable, and we are allowed to be innovative, as indicated by the transformation of Judaism from Abraham to Moses, from the prophets to the priests, from the Talmudic world and the rabbinate to its modern manifestations.

Today, most secular Jews are isolated individuals full of doubt, and many are ambivalent about being Jewish. Even within some of the mainstream denominations, the question on everyone's lips is, "What is a viable unifier and stabilizer for (secular) Jewish identity?" For secular Judaism, the answer lies in providing a new narrative and new forms of community that permit contact between individual subjectivity and Jewish traditions without the xenophobia and alienation generated by the religious categories of purity, impurity, divine election, and divine protection.

Secular Judaism, whether agnostic or atheistic, is rooted in the rational, humanistic, and scientific culture of our time. It is an excellent antidote to irrationalism, dogmatism, and authoritarianism. Nevertheless, we should recognize that rationalism is limited in its ability to fulfill the emotional needs that connect people and groups. The search for meaning and the creation of social ties include dimensions that are found outside the sphere of rationality, bound up as they are in rites, ceremonies, and spaces of coexistence where people can share collective sentiments.

It has been almost a century since the great philosopher Martin Buber called our attention to the difference between religion and religiosity/spirituality. While the former refers to the institutionalized dimensions of religious life, the latter expresses a personal search for transcendence and connection with the universe. For Buber, religion does not necessitate religiosity, just as the expression of religiosity/spirituality does not need religious institutions. It is no coincidence that Buber attended synagogue with assiduous infrequency.

A similar sentiment was expressed by Albert Einstein in *Religion and Science*:

> The religious geniuses of all ages have been distinguished by this kind of religious feeling, which knows no dogma and no God conceived in man's image; so that there can be no Church whose central teachings are based on it. Hence it is precisely among the heretics of every age that we find men who were filled with the highest kind of religious

feeling and were in many cases regarded by their contemporaries as Atheists, sometimes also as saints. [. . .] You will hardly find one among the profounder sort of scientific minds without a peculiar religious feeling of his own. But it is different from the religion of the naive man. For the latter God is a being from whose care one hopes to benefit and whose punishment one fears; a sublimation of a feeling similar to that of a child for its father, a being to whom one stands to some extent in a personal relation, however deeply it may be tinged with awe. [. . .] There is nothing divine about morality; it is a purely human affair.

This distinction is fundamental because it is the basis of a humanistic view of religion, a view already present in the great mystical traditions. Spiritual experience is a personal path that must not be confused with rites or transferred to some external power or formal institution. The search for life's transcendental or spiritual meaning is always a personally constructed path. It cannot be transformed into truths to be imposed on others.

The need for spirituality has not ceased to exist even in individualized and secularized democratic societies. But what do we mean by spirituality? It is something of value for which one is ready to risk one's life, since in its absence life has no meaning. It is what gives vital force and basic meaning to our lives.

The tragedy of spirituality is that it is easily converted into its opposite, fanaticism. Fanaticism destroys our ability to respect what is sacred to others, and when taken to extremes, it justifies the destruction of others because their belief system is different. For spirituality to prevail, the fundamental tenet of respect for individual liberty must exist —allowing each person to express his or her own beliefs without imposing those beliefs on others.

Humanistic Judaism must not be reduced to simple rationalism and naturalism. It must provide answers to the subjective dramas of the people it seeks to serve. It should produce new *drashot* (interpretations) of Judaism that point the way toward innovative individual and communal practices. To say it will be a clean break with the past is impossible and self-destructive because, for the humanistic Jew, one's sense of Jewishness is a willful expression that upholds collective memory, even if only familial. In this regard, every Jew is a traditionalist. What matters is the meaning each individual gives to tradition and the past.

Secular Judaism should provide a welcoming, innovative format for ceremonies and rituals but should not become a new theological movement. Secular Jews should not be afraid to absorb cultural elements from the past when these elements are in accordance with their individual affinities. Those who circumcise their sons or give their children *b'nai mitzvoth* ceremonies do so as an affirmation of tradition, not religious edict. In the same way, most secular Jews do not recite the *Kaddish* at the burial or wake of a loved one because they believe the words they utter. They do it because it was recited by their parents, grandparents, great-grandparents, and so on. It is a way to make contact with one's ancestors, just as one might recite *Shema Yisrael* (seminal Jewish prayer that says, "Hear, O Israel! The Lord is our God! The Lord is One!").

These are rituals that may allow for a connection to the past and its collective memories.

At the same time, humanistic Judaism should be vigilant in its efforts to overcome components of Talmudic Judaism that from a contemporary perspective are offensive to the humanistic sensibility, which sanctifies both life and the individual but never collective identities. Humanistic Judaism is a Judaism that moves beyond the categories of pure and impure in its treatment of individuals and groups.

All of this does not dismiss the problem of defining who is Jewish from an institutional point of view. Every organized group defines its membership rules through rites of passage. Talmudic Judaism resolved this problem by reducing it to biological destiny or acceptance via rites of conversion. Although Judaism with clearly defined matrilineal borders is displeasing to most humanistic Jews, it does provide a sense of security for some. For Jews of all stripes, the existing rules of entry are often seen as poor or regrettable, yet they assure a familiar order.

Because every club has its own admission rules, old members will probably find it difficult to accept new criteria. Yet contemporary Judaism is a vast cultural field with porous borders, and that is a good thing. More than a decade ago, a rabbi from the Conservative movement, Jack Wertheimer, announced that Reform Judaism's decision to accept patrilineage would divide Judaism. He was wrong; Judaism did not become divided. To remain united, Judaism should coalesce around the lowest—not the highest—common denominator.

If Judaism opens up to the world, who will define who is Jewish and who is not? How do we know if someone is or is not part of the "club"? I believe this is a false problem, a red herring, especially in the Diaspora, where identity cards are not issued by Jewish communities.

Those who do not believe in welcoming non-Jews who choose Judaism may fear an overwhelming wave of eager converts. This fear became ingrained over the centuries by Christian and Muslim prohibitions on Jewish proselytism. Yet there is no such risk of massive invasion on the horizon. An exclusionary Judaism does not guarantee the future of Judaism. It guarantees only that Judaism will exclude a growing number of Jews.

The question of conversion has different implications in Israel and in the Diaspora. In Israel, it is defined as the right to citizenship, and it mobilizes economic and political interests that do not exist in the Diaspora. The State of Israel holds a demographic interest in expanding its population, and this has led to extremely broad acceptance of immigrants. As we have already seen, the problem with this is that the immigrant must later endure problems caused by the legal control of the ultra-Orthodox rabbis who define nationality as it appears on identity cards. The solution under discussion in Israel has to do with the state's right to define the rules by which it would grant Jewish nationality to people who are not religious.

Humanistic Judaism must be open to Jews-by-choice as well as Jews-by-birth. Talmudic Judaism transformed the Jewish body into something pure and the non-Jew into something impure. Whatever the justifications may have been, they are unacceptable from a modern perspective. Humanistic Judaism should create rituals for becoming Jewish that do not demand declarations of religious belief. Jews would be those who identify with Judaism, be it by birth, by having a Jewish father or mother, or for non-Jews, by deciding to marry a Jew and build a Jewish family for one's children. Furthermore, descendants of Jews who at some moment in the past were converted by force should now be able to reclaim their Jewish identity and be "naturally" Jewish.

This new reality drives the insecurities of those who seek to limit the number of members in the tribe of Einstein and Freud. Belonging to an exclusive club makes people feel special, but the price of excluding others will lead to the demographic extinction and cultural impoverishment of the Jewish people.

A more open Judaism brings its own challenges and redefines Judaism as we know it. This redefinition is already taking place, and everywhere we look there are people creating Judaisms with multiple faces and multiple interfaces with the world. They are creating cultural spaces that join people together without the weight of destiny. It is no longer vital to be tied to Judaism by birth—though Jewish parentage will continue to play a central role, as it does for all ethnic identities.

Humanistic Judaism's main struggle is to find a way create communities. Some may develop in partnership with humanistic Jewish religious organizations; others may develop separately, via the Internet, humanistic synagogues, cultural centers, schools, or secular *yeshivot*. Without organization, humanistic Jews will remain hostage to the diverse currents of religious Judaism vis-à-vis rites of passage (births, *b'nai mitzvoth*, burials, conversions, holidays, and commemorations).

Today there are many creative institutional initiatives that support the cause of humanistic secular Judaism. Among them are the Centre Communautaire Laïc Juif in Brussels; the YOK group in Buenos Aires; Alma Hebrew College; Oranim; the Avi Chai Foundation; Elul, the Bina Center for Jewish Identity and Hebrew Culture (which includes a secular yeshiva), and Tmura—the Institute for Training Secular Humanistic Rabbis & Jewish Leadership in Israel; the congregations of the Society for Humanistic Judaism, founded by Rabbi Sherwin Wine; the International Institute for Secular Humanistic Judaism (providing educational programs and training humanistic rabbis); the Workmen's Circle/ Arbeter Ring (secular Yiddish tradition) in the United States; the French Association pour un Judaïsme Humaniste et Laïque; the Center for Cultural Judaism (supports college and university courses for Jewish secularization); the International Federation for Secular & Humanistic Judaism (umbrella organization of the world-wide Movement), and journals such as *Yahadut Chofshit* (Free Judaism), *Plurielles,* and *Contemplate.*

A new *drash* on Jewish tradition has enormous potential for creativity and renewal. It is being developed in part by Reform, Reconstructionist and Conservative rabbis, but it remains limited by their institutional attachments and theistic orientation. For example, on Yom Kippur, the Day of Atonement, religious tradition expects Jews to ask God to forgive them for wrong acts committed during the previous year. The idea of asking for forgiveness from God, who will inscribe our names in the "Book of Life," is infantile and immoral. It is infantile because it transfers to a higher force, to an omnipotent father, the power of absolution and the ultimate responsibility for our actions. It is immoral because it assumes, as in Catholic confession, that evil can be periodically erased by divine decree rather than by our own reparative actions. Yom Kippur could be reassigned a healing meaning, one of self-forgiveness for blaming ourselves too much. It could help free us from the guilt we carry for living in a world full of injustice and suffering.

Similarly, our vision of what it is to be kosher (pure) and *treif* (impure) or of the meaning of *mitzvah* (commandment) could be recreated in terms of conduct that seems ethically correct or incorrect. In today's popular parlance, this is exactly the kind of meaning that predominates: *mitzvah* refers to an act of human kindness, the product of a personal initiative, not a divine commandment. *Treif* has come to mean simply something that is wrong or illegal.

Secular Judaism should celebrate the Jewish condition as a source of joy. While it should never forget historical experiences of persecution and suffering, it should include elements of self-help and celebrate its own identity without promoting narcissistic, ethnocentric views. The new ways of celebrating Judaism, in all of its manifestations, should be centered on providing support for people to make them feel proud of their Judaism ("Jews are Jewcy"), helping them value happiness and humor, encouraging them to look to the past for wisdom in uncertain times.

Although it will be increasingly centered on individual subjective needs, solidarity with Jews under duress will continue to be one of the foundations of Jewish identity. At the same time, anti-Semitism cannot continue to be presented as an inescapable destiny, nor should it be associated, implicitly or explicitly, with a discourse or feeling that viscerally separates Jews from non-Jews.

Identification with the State of Israel will continue to be a pillar of identity for most secular Jews, but this should not imply blind support of the Israeli government. In fact, humanistic Jews may have an important role to play in cooperating with peace movements in Israel, even if that role includes openly criticizing Israeli policy when necessary.

Secular Humanistic Jews should value the positive aspects of the Diaspora and preserve the memory of the Holocaust without feeding paranoia or a sense of victimhood. They should absorb the best of rabbinical tradition without submitting to anachronistic values and practices. The desire to uphold tradition should be affirmed on its own terms, not defined by xenophobia or the ghost of anti-Semitism. Secular Humanistic Jews should transform destiny into freedom, uniting tradition with renewal.

The decision to live as a Humanistic Jew is an individual and collective adventure that has no godgiven guarantees.

How and when will secular Jews return to social movements capable of renewing Judaism? The first generations of humanistic Jews defined themselves in reaction to their parents, who had Orthodox Judaism as a reference point, a system of rigid values that did not respond to the challenges and expectations of the modern world. Today, a good portion of young humanistic Jews do not have any clear Jewish reference point to help them define their objectives.

The process of reconstructing humanistic secular Judaism will not be the work of individual intellectuals. In the best of cases, their contribution will be to deconstruct the dogmas and straightjackets that were once acceptable but that today are barriers to the development of a new vision. The new humanistic Judaism will be the product of the younger generation. The generation now leaving the scene has the responsibility to support and facilitate this transition, because even if we do not have a clear model to offer, we must still pass on our knowledge and experience. In the end, each generation is responsible for what it makes of its legacy.

Appendix: World Jewish Population

Assessing the world Jewish population is a tricky issue. Demographic counting cannot be dissociated from the self-definition of contemporary Jews. In many countries, but not in the United States, the national census includes religious affiliation. Many Jews, however, do not define themselves as Jewish by religion.

According to the American Jewish Identity Survey, conducted in 2001 by Egon Mayer, Barry Kosmin, and Ariela Keysar, the number of persons of Jewish origin in the United States was 7.7 million, an increase of 900,000 in relation to 1990. During the same period, the number of people who self-defined as Jews decreased from 5.5 million to 5.3 million. Around half of this total defined themselves as "secular," and 48 percent did not belong to any Jewish organization. Half of the marriages in the 1990s were to a non-Jewish spouse.

This data is confirmed by Barry A. Kosmin's paper *The Changing Population Profile of American*

Jews, 1990–2008, which shows that from 1990 to 2008 Jews with no religion increased steadily from 20 to 37 percent of the total. Around half of the American Jewish population has only one Jewish parent.

Another interesting example is that of Argentina. In 1960, the national census asked people's religion, and 310,000 respondents answered Jewish. From that year onward, tens of thousands emigrated due to economic hardship or political persecution. According to the data presented below, collected by Sergio DellaPergola and used by the Jewish People Policy Planning Institute in Jerusalem, the number of Argentine Jews in 2009 was 182,500. However, research conducted in 2004 under the auspices of the Joint Distribution Committee, which used a broader definition of Jewishness that included having one Jewish parent, indicated that in the city of Buenos Aires alone there were 244,000 Jews, and 300,000 in Argentina as a whole. Of the total of self-defined Jews, 33 percent were born to a Jewish mother and 39 percent to a Jewish father. As a result of these findings, the Joint Distribution Committee began an outreach project aimed at "peripheral" Jews.

The following table and map (based on the DellaPergola data) represent the distribution of the world Jewish population. They reflect the lowest figures available and are useful in establishing a baseline for the challenge we face, that of reaching out to the fifty to eighty percent of individuals who have not yet found a place in Judaism.

World Jewish Population, 2009 (Core Definition)

Country	Jewish Population	
North America		
Canada	375,000	
United States	5,275,000	
Total North America		5,650,000
Central America		
Bahamas	300	
Costa Rica	2,500	
Cuba	500	
Dominican Republic	100	
El Salvador	100	
Guatemala	900	
Jamaica	300	
Mexico	39,500	
Netherlands Antilles	200	
Panama	8,000	
Puerto Rico	1,500	
Virgin Islands	500	
Other	300	

Total Central America		54,700

South America

Argentina	182,500	
Bolivia	500	
Brazil	95,800	
Chile	20,600	
Colombia	2,700	
Ecuador	900	
Paraguay	900	
Peru	2,000	
Suriname	200	
Uruguay	17,600	
Venezuela	12,200	
Total South America		335,900
Total		6,040,600

European Union

Austria	9,000
Belgium	30,400
Bulgaria	2,000
Czech Republic	3,900
Denmark	6,400
Estonia	1,900
Finland	1,100
France	485,000
Germany	120,000
Greece	4,500
Hungary	48,800
Ireland	1,200
Italy	28,500

Latvia	10,000	
Lithuania	3,300	
Luxembourg	600	
Netherlands	30,000	
Poland	3,200	
Portugal	500	
Romania	9,800	
Slovakia	2,600	
Slovenia	100	
Spain	12,000	
Sweden	15,000	
United Kingdom	293,000	
Other	100	
Total Eur. Union		1,122,900

Other Western Europe

Gibraltar	600	
Norway	1,200	
Switzerland	17,700	
Total other W. Europe		19,500

Eastern Europe

Belarus	16,800	
Moldova	4,200	
Russia	210,000	
Ukraine	74,000	
Total FSU Republics	305,000	
Bosnia-Herzegovina	500	
Croatia	1,700	
Macedonia	100	
Serbia	1,400	
Turkey	17,700	

Other	100	
Total other E. Europe and Balkans		21,500
Total		1,468,900

Asia

Israel	5,287,200	
West Bank	282,000	
Total Israel and West Bank		5,569,200

Armenia	0	
Azerbaijan	6,500	
Georgia	3,300	
Kazakhstan	3,800	
Kyrgyzstan	700	
Tajikistan	0	
Turkmenistan	200	
Uzbekistan	4,700	
Total former USSR in Asia		19,200

China	1,500
India	5,000
Iran	10,500
Japan	1,000
Korea, South	100
Philippines	100
Singapore	300
Syria	100
Taiwan	100
Thailand	200
Yemen	200
Other	200

Total other Asia		19,300
Total		5,607,700
Africa		
Egypt	100	
Ethiopia	100	
Morocco	2,800	
Tunisia	1,000	
Other	0	
Total North Africa		4,000
Botswana	100	
Congo D.R.	100	
Kenya	400	
Namibia	100	
Nigeria	100	
South Africa	71,000	
Zimbabwe	400	
Other	300	
Total other Africa		72,500
Total		76,500
Oceania		
Australia	107,500	
New Zealand	7,500	
Other	100	
Total		115,100

Source: Sergio DellaPergola, Shlomo Argov Chair in Israel-Diaspora Relations, Hebrew University of Jerusalem.

MAP OF THE WORLD JEWISH POPULATION - 2009

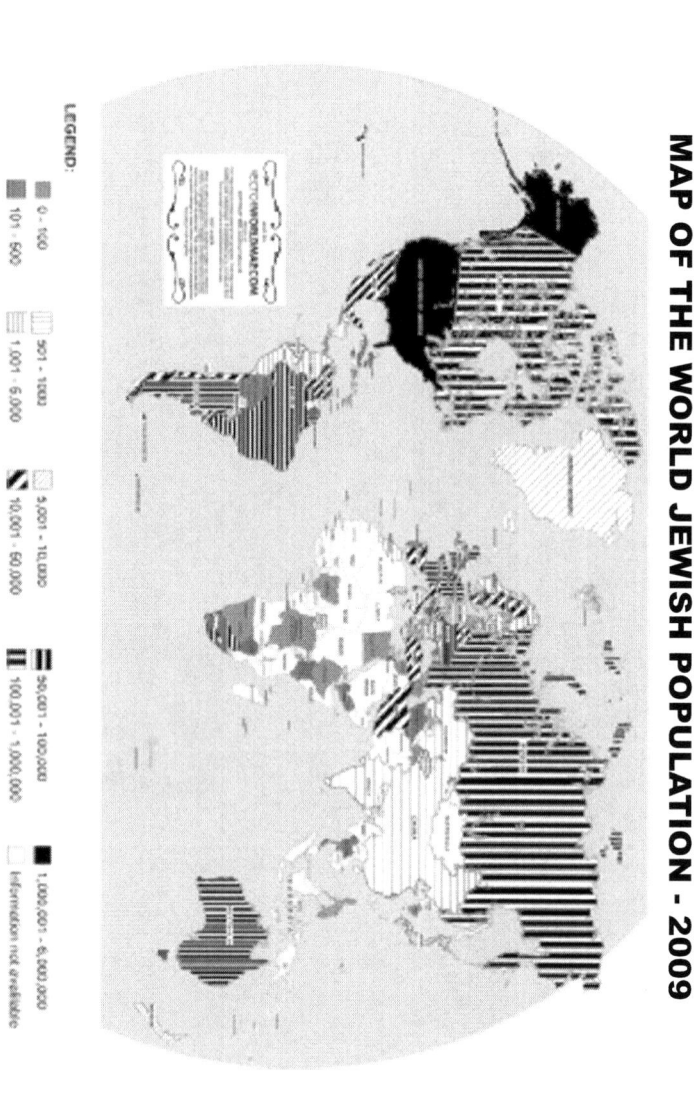

Glossary

· *Am ha'aretz* ("people of the land"): Common people, the ignorant.

· *Apikoires*: Heretics. Used to describe Jews sympathetic to Greek philosophy: literally, followers of the philosopher Epicurus. Now used to describe "heretical" freethinkers.

· *Ashkenazim*: Most Jews who settled in Germany, Austria, and Central and Eastern Europe.

· *Asmachta*: Fragments of biblical text used to support a rabbinical interpretation.

· *Beit Knesset* ("meeting house"): Synagogue.

· *Beit Midrash* ("house of interpretation"): House of study.

· *B'nai mitzvoth*: bar/bat mitzvahs

· *Cherem*: Rabbinical court decision by which a community member is banned and prohibited from all contact with other Jews; the Jewish equivalent to excommunication.

· *Chutzpah*: Impertinence, insolence, gall.

· *Dina d'malchuta dina*: Talmudic principle: "the law of the land is the law."

· *Drash*: Interpretation.

- *Elohim*: One of the names of God in the Bible; it is grammatically plural.
- *Galut*: Exile.
- *Gemarah*: Body of canonical rabbinic interpretations based on the *Mishnah*.
- *Ger*: The stranger among us, the convert, the Jew by choice who generally follows the values and customs of Judaism.
- *Goyim* (singular, *goy*): *Goy* is the Hebrew word for a people, including the Jewish people. *Goyim* is the plural. It is the term for non-Jews used in the Talmud.
- *Halakhah*: Body of religious laws and practices that must be followed according to the rabbinical-Talmudic tradition.
- Chanukah: Commemorates the liberation of the Temple during the Maccabean revolt against the Hellenistic kingdom of the Seleucids.
- *Hanukia*: Eight-branched candelabrum used during the festival of Chanukah.
- *Haredim* (singular *Haredi*; "fearers of God"): Ultra-Orthodox Jews.
- *Kaddish*: Prayer for the memory of the dead.
- Karaites: Jewish group (originating in Mesopotamia between the seventh and ninth centuries CE) that denied the sacredness of the Talmud.
- *Kavanah*: Intention.
- *Ketuvim*: Writings (title of the final section of the Bible).
- *Kol Nidre*: Opening prayer of Yom Kippur, the Day of Atonement.
- Kosher: Food classed according to the dietary

laws of pure and impure. More broadly, it is used as a slang expression meaning correct or acceptable.

· Noachide Covenant: Pact that God made with Noah and humankind in which he promised never to destroy all life again and, in return, demanded obedience to seven ethical commandments — including the prohibition of murder.

· *Mi-de-rabbanan*: Rules developed by rabbis without direct support from the biblical text.

· *Midrash Haggadah*: Narrative interpretations, anecdotes.

· *Midrash Halakhah*: Interpretations having to do with the *mitzvoth*/commandments.

· *Minhagim*: Customs.

· *Minyan*: A quorum of ten Jews (males according to Orthodoxy, both sexes in other denominations) needed for communal prayer and various religious ceremonies.

· *Mishnah*: First group of rabbinical interpretations of the Bible; comprises six volumes.

· *Mishneh Torah*: Compendium of rabbinical laws compiled by Maimonides; continues to be a major reference work to this day.

· *Mizrahim*: Jews who settled in the Arab world.

· *Mitzvah* (plural *mitzvoth*): Divine commandment.

· *Nevi'im*: Prophets.

· *Ohr lagoyim*: "Light unto the nations."

· Pardes ("orchard"): Acronym of *Pshat* (the simple text), *Remez* (what the text suggests), *Drash* (search or interpretation), and *Sod* (secret, the mystical dimension).

- *Pirkei Avot* ("Ethics [Chapters] of the Fathers"): Book included in the Mishnah.
- *Pshat*: Simple, literal meaning.
- Purim: Festival that commemorates Queen Esther's intervention before the Persian King Ahasuerus in order to annul the edict of his chief adviser, Haman, who had plotted to eliminate all Jews in the kingdom.
- *Remez*: What the text suggests or implies.
- Rosh Hashanah: Jewish New Year.
- Sanhedrin: Greco-Roman-era assembly of priests and scholars with legislative and judicial powers.
- *Sephardim*: Descendants of Jewish communities from the Islamic world, including those who lived in Christian Spain until the expulsion of the Jews in 1492.
- *Shabbat*: The Sabbath; weekly day of rest.
- *Shema Yisrael*: Seminal Jewish Prayer found in the Bible: "Hear, O Israel! The Lord is our God! The Lord is One!"
- *Shulkhan Arukh*: Codification of rabbinical laws compiled by Joseph Caro in the sixteenth century; considered to be the primary reference work treating questions of Halakhah.
- *Sod*: The Kabbalistic, secret, mystical dimension of the biblical text.
- Talmud: Body of writings consisting of the Mishnah and the Gemarah.
- *Tanach*: The Bible, which comprises three separate groups of writings: Torah (Pentateuch), *Nevi'im* (Prophets), and *Ketuvim* (Writings). The word *Tanach* is an acronym for the names of the three groups.

- *Tefutsoth*: Diaspora.
- Torah: Pentateuch.
- *Torah sheb'alpeh*: The oral Torah, the interpretations of the biblical text.
- *Torah shebikhtav*: The written Torah; in particular, the Pentateuch and, in general, the Bible.
- *Treif*: Impure or not kosher
- Yeshiva (plural *yeshivot*): Centers for religious studies and rabbinical training.
- *Yidn* (singular *yid*): In Yiddish, the Jews.
- Yiddish: Germanic language that contains many Eastern European and Hebrew expressions and is written in Hebrew letters. Yiddish was the *lingua franca* of nearly all Eastern European Jews.
- Yom Kippur: Day of Atonement, the most sacred holiday of the year.

Acknowledgments

Judaism, as an existential problem and source of reflection, has accompanied me throughout my life. I have been lucky enough to share this long journey with many people, without whom this book would not exist. It would not be realistic to list all of them here, and my memory would certainly fail me. All I can do is mention some of the milestones at which I met many of them: the IMI movement, a Latin American creation of the 1960s that sought to synthesize Zionism with the revolutionary spirit of the era; the pacifist student group IESH, which mobilized Israeli Arabs and Jews and Latin American and European immigrants and which, in 1972, emerged victorious in the elections of the student association at the University of Haifa, a singular event in Israeli history; the instructors of the Jewish history program at the University of Haifa, who renewed my vision of the subject; and the academic world in general, perhaps the only truly cosmopolitan community, where I have met so many colleagues who possess tremendous humane qualities.

The exchange of ideas with Salomon Wald, whose vision of Judaism and the world are quite different from mine, was always a great source of intellectual stimulation. My dialogue and friendship of several decades with Rabbi Nilton Bonder influenced me greatly as I worked out my vision of Judaism. Bila Sorj's and Michael Leigh's detailed commentary on an early draft certainly improved much in this text. The comments and encouragement I received from Marvin Rosenblum on the English edition were invaluable. Of course, none of them are responsible for my opinions and mistakes. Finally, I want recognize the support I have received from the Edelstein Center for Social Research and in particular its president, my friend Joel Edelstein.

For Further Reading on Humanistic Judaism...[1]

Abramson, Glenda. ed. *The Experienced Soul: Studies in Amichai*. Boulder, CO: Westview, 1997.

Aleichem, Sholem. *The Best of Sholem Aleichem*. Irving Howe and Ruth Wisse, eds. Washington, DC: New Republic, 1979.

Amichai, Yehuda. *Even a Fist Was Once an Open Palm with Fingers: Recent Poems*. Translated by Benjamin and Barbara Harshav. New York: Harper Perennial, 1991.

Arendt, Hannah. *Rahel Varnhagen: The Life of a Jewess*. Liliane Weissberg, ed. Translated by Richard and Clara Winston. Baltimore, MD: Johns Hopkins University Press, 1997.

Bar-Zohar, Michael. *The Armed Prophet: A Biography of Ben Gurion*. Translated by Len Ortzen. London: Barker, 1967.

Bauer, Yehuda. *Rethinking the Holocaust*. New Haven, CT: Yale University Press, 2001.

Bendor, Shunya. *The Social Structure of Ancient Israel: The Institution of the Family from the Settlement to the End of the Monarchy*. Jerusalem: Simor, 1996.

---

[1] Several people have contributed to the compendium that follows, though it is primarily drawn from the bibliography organized by Rabbi Adam Chalom to complement *Judaism in a Secular Age: An Anthology of Secular Humanistic Jewish Thought* (Milan, KS: IISHJ/Milan Press, 1995).

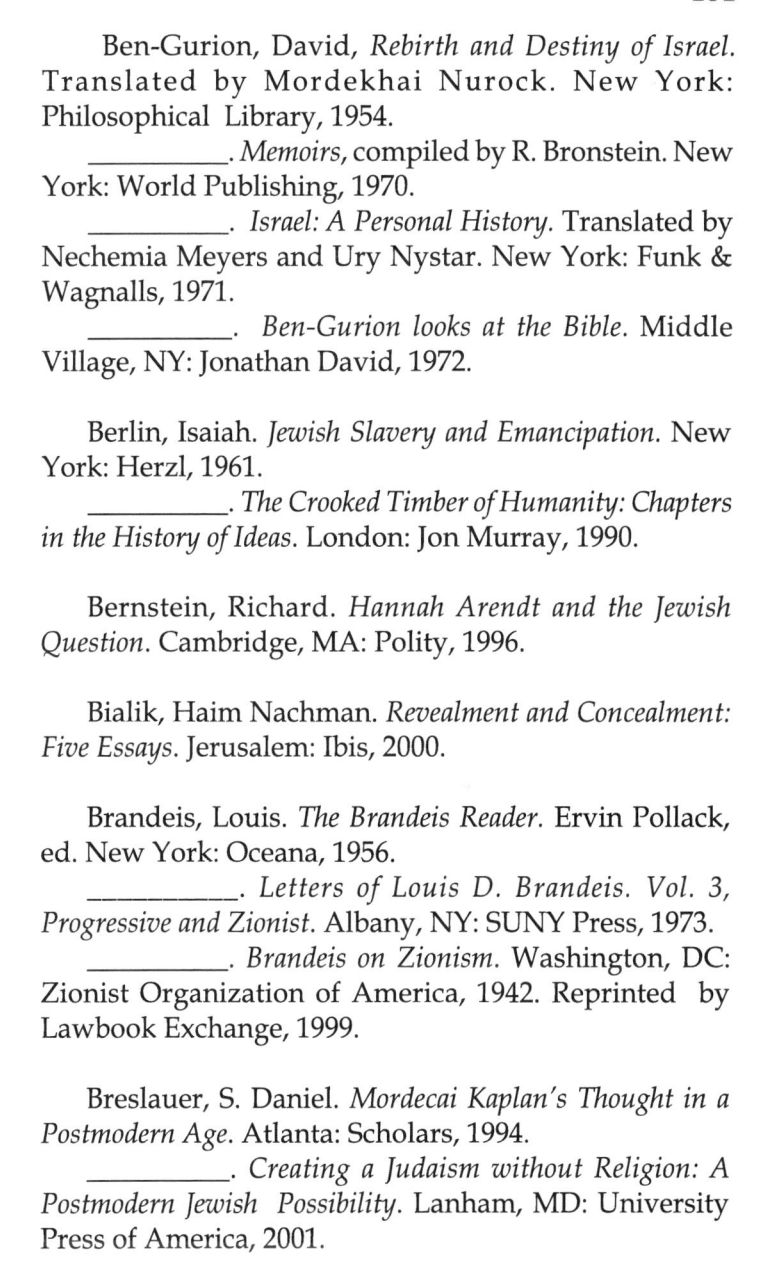

Ben-Gurion, David, *Rebirth and Destiny of Israel.* Translated by Mordekhai Nurock. New York: Philosophical Library, 1954.
_____. *Memoirs*, compiled by R. Bronstein. New York: World Publishing, 1970.
_____. *Israel: A Personal History.* Translated by Nechemia Meyers and Ury Nystar. New York: Funk & Wagnalls, 1971.
_____. *Ben-Gurion looks at the Bible.* Middle Village, NY: Jonathan David, 1972.

Berlin, Isaiah. *Jewish Slavery and Emancipation.* New York: Herzl, 1961.
_____. *The Crooked Timber of Humanity: Chapters in the History of Ideas.* London: Jon Murray, 1990.

Bernstein, Richard. *Hannah Arendt and the Jewish Question.* Cambridge, MA: Polity, 1996.

Bialik, Haim Nachman. *Revealment and Concealment: Five Essays.* Jerusalem: Ibis, 2000.

Brandeis, Louis. *The Brandeis Reader.* Ervin Pollack, ed. New York: Oceana, 1956.
_____. *Letters of Louis D. Brandeis. Vol. 3, Progressive and Zionist.* Albany, NY: SUNY Press, 1973.
_____. *Brandeis on Zionism.* Washington, DC: Zionist Organization of America, 1942. Reprinted by Lawbook Exchange, 1999.

Breslauer, S. Daniel. *Mordecai Kaplan's Thought in a Postmodern Age.* Atlanta: Scholars, 1994.
_____. *Creating a Judaism without Religion: A Postmodern Jewish Possibility.* Lanham, MD: University Press of America, 2001.

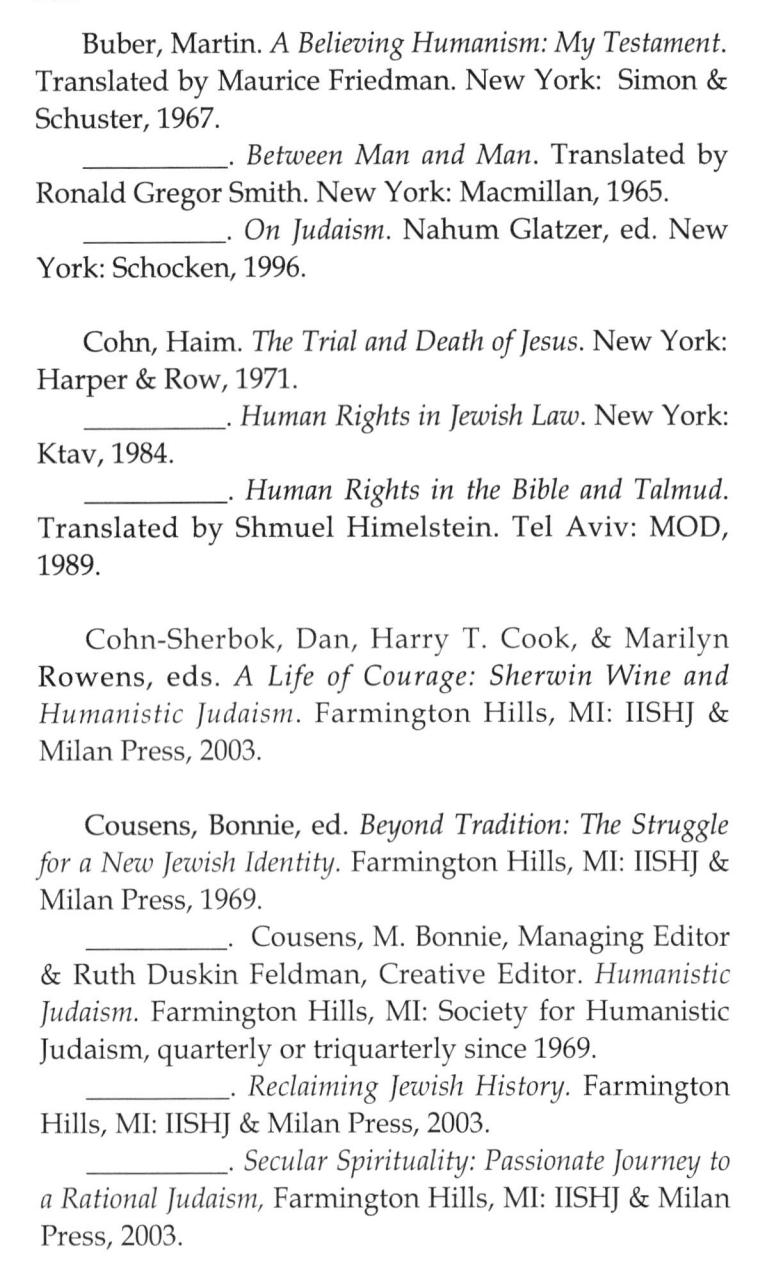

Buber, Martin. *A Believing Humanism: My Testament.* Translated by Maurice Friedman. New York: Simon & Schuster, 1967.

_____. *Between Man and Man.* Translated by Ronald Gregor Smith. New York: Macmillan, 1965.

_____. *On Judaism.* Nahum Glatzer, ed. New York: Schocken, 1996.

Cohn, Haim. *The Trial and Death of Jesus.* New York: Harper & Row, 1971.

_____. *Human Rights in Jewish Law.* New York: Ktav, 1984.

_____. *Human Rights in the Bible and Talmud.* Translated by Shmuel Himelstein. Tel Aviv: MOD, 1989.

Cohn-Sherbok, Dan, Harry T. Cook, & Marilyn Rowens, eds. *A Life of Courage: Sherwin Wine and Humanistic Judaism.* Farmington Hills, MI: IISHJ & Milan Press, 2003.

Cousens, Bonnie, ed. *Beyond Tradition: The Struggle for a New Jewish Identity.* Farmington Hills, MI: IISHJ & Milan Press, 1969.

_____. Cousens, M. Bonnie, Managing Editor & Ruth Duskin Feldman, Creative Editor. *Humanistic Judaism.* Farmington Hills, MI: Society for Humanistic Judaism, quarterly or triquarterly since 1969.

_____. *Reclaiming Jewish History.* Farmington Hills, MI: IISHJ & Milan Press, 2003.

_____. *Secular Spirituality: Passionate Journey to a Rational Judaism,* Farmington Hills, MI: IISHJ & Milan Press, 2003.

Deutscher, Isaac. *The Non-Jewish Jew and Other Essays.* Tamara Deutscher, ed. New York: Oxford University Press, 1968.

Dubnova-Erlikh, Sofia. *The Life and Work of S. M. Dubnov: Diaspora, Nationalism, and Jewish History.* Bloomington, IN: Indiana University Press, 1991.

Dubnow, Simon. *An Outline of Jewish History.* New York: M. N. Maisel, 1929.

_____. *History of the Jews in Russia and Poland from the Earliest Times until the Present Day.* New Jersey: Ktav, 1975.

Einstein, Albert. *About Zionism.* London: Soncino, 1930.

_____. *Essays in Humanism.* New York: Philosophical Library, 1983.

Elon, Amos. *Herzl.* New York: Holt, Rinehart and Winston, 1975.

Epstein, Greg M. *Good Without God: What a Billion Nonreligious People Do Believe.* New York: William Morrow, 2009.

Feldman, Rond, ed. *The Jew as Pariah: Jewish Identity and Politics in the Modern Age.* New York: Grove, 1978.

Freud, Sigmund, *Freud and Judaism.* David Meghnazi, ed. London: Karnac, 1993.

Friedman, Daniel. *Jews without Judaism.* Buffalo, NY: Prometheus, 2002.

Gay, Peter. *A Godless Jew: Freud, Atheism, and the Making of Psychoanalysis.* New Haven, CT: Yale University Press, 1987.

Gitelman, Zvi. *Religion or Ethnicity: Jewish Identities in Evolution*. New Brunswick, NJ: Rutgers University Press: 2009.

Goldfinger, Eva. *Basic Ideas of Secular Humanistic Judaism*. IISHJ: 1998.

Goodman, Saul, ed. *The Faith of Secular Jews*. New Jersey: Ktav, 1976.

Gresser, Moshe. *Dual Allegiance: Freud as a Modern Jew*. Albany, NY: SUNY Press, 1994.

Herzl, Theodor. *Old-New Land*. Translated by Lotta Levensohn. New York: Bloch, 1960.

_____. *Complete Diaries*. New York: Herzl, 1960.

_____. *Zionist Writings, Essays, and Addresses*. Translated by Harry Zohn. New York: Herzl, 1973.

Horn, Bernard. *Facing the Fires: Conversations with A. B. Yehoshua*. Syracuse, NY: Syracuse University Press, 1997.

Ibry, David. *Exodus to Humanism: Jewish Identity without Religion*. Prometheus, 1999.

Ignatieff, Michael. *Isaiah Berlin: A Life*. New York: Metropolitan, 1998.

Kafka, Franz, *Franz Kafka's Letter to His Father*. Translated by Ernst Kaiser and Eithne Wilkins. Revised by Arthur S. Wensinger. Retrieved from <http://www.kafka-franz.com/KAFKA-letter.htm>.

Kaplan, Mordecai. *Dynamic Judaism: The Essential Writings of Mordecai M. Kaplan*. New York: Schocken/Reconstructionist, 1985.

_____. *The Greater Judaism in the Making: A Study of the Modern Evolution of Judaism.* New York: Reconstructionist, 1960.

_____. *Judaism without Super-naturalism: The Only Alternative to Orthodoxy and Secularism.* New York: Reconstructionist, 1958.

_____. *The Meaning of God in Modern Jewish Religion.* Detroit: Wayne State University Press, 1994.

Katz, Zev. *From the Gestapo to the Gulags: One Jewish Life.* Portland, OR: Vallentine Mitchell, 2004.

Kogel, Renee and Zev Katz, eds. *Judaism in a Secular Age: An Anthology of Secular Humanistic Jewish Thought.* Milan, KS: IISHJ/Milan Press, 1995.

Kornberg, Jacques. *Theodor Herzl: From Assimilation to Zionism.* Bloomington: Indiana University Press, 1993

Levy, Karen. *The Early Modern European Roots of Secular Humanistic Jewish Thought.* Milan, KS: IISHJ/Milan Press, 1995.

Malkin, Yaakov. *What Do Secular Jews Believe?* Jerusalem: Free Judaism, 1998.

_____. *Secular Judaism: Faith, Values, and Spirituality.* Portland, OR: Vallentine Mitchell, 2004.

_____. *Judaism without God? Judaism as Culture and Bible as Literature.* Translated by Shmuel Gertel. Milan, KS: Library of Secular Judaism/Milan Press, 2007

_____. *Epicurus and Apikorsim: The Influence of the Greek Epicurus and Jewish Apikorsim on Judaism.* Milan, KS: Library of Secular Judaism/Milan Press, 2007.

Mazor, Yair. *Somber Lust: The Art of Amos Oz*. Albany, NY: SUNY Press, 2002.

Mendes-Flohr, Paul, ed. *Martin Buber: A Contemporary Perspective*. Syracuse, NY, and Jerusalem: Syracuse University Press and the Israel Academy of Arts and Sciences, 2002.

Memmi, Albert. *The Liberation of the Jew*. Translated by Judy Hyun. New York: Orion, 1966.

Miron, Dan. *Bialik and the Prophetic Mode in Modern Hebrew Poetry*. Syracuse, NY: Syracuse University Press, 2000.

_____. *The Image of the Shtetl and Other Studies of Modern Jewish Literary Imagination*. Syracuse, NY: Syracuse University Press, 2000.

Moore, Donald. *Martin Buber: Prophet of Religious Secularism*. New York: Fordham University Press, 1996.

Muraskin, Bennett. *Humanist Readings in Jewish Folklore*. Milan, KS: IISHJ/Milan Press, 2001.

_____. *Let Justice Well Up Like Water: Progressive Jews from Hillel to Helen Suzman*. Richmond Heights, OH, and New York: CSJO/Center for Cultural Judaism, 2004.

Oz, Amos. *In the Land of Israel*. Translated by Maurie Goldberg-Bartura. San Diego: Harcourt Brace Jovanovich, 1983.

_____. *A Tale of Love and Darkness*. Orland, FL: Harcourt, 2003.

_____. *How to Cure a Fanatic*. Princeton, NJ: Princeton University Press, 2006.

Ring, Jennifer. *The Political Consequences of Thinking: Gender and Judaism in the Work of Hannah Arendt.* Albany, NY: SUNY Press, 1997.

Rosenfeld, Max. *Festivals, Folklore, and Philosophy: A Secularist Revisits Jewish Traditions.* Philadelphia, PA: Sholem Aleichem Club, 1997.

_____. Editor and translator of *A Union for Shabbos and Other Stories of Jewish Life in America.* Philadelphia, PA: Sholem Aleichem Club Press, 1967.

_____. Editor and translator of *Pushcarts and Dreamers.* Philadelphia, PA: Sholem Aleichem Club, 1993.

Schappes, Morris. *A Documentary History of the Jews in the United States, 1654–1875.* New York: Schocken, 1971.

Scult, Mel. *Judaism Faces the Twentieth Century: A Biography of Mordecai Kaplan.* Detroit: Wayne State University Press, 1993.

Seid, Judith. *God-Optional Judaism: Alternatives for Cultural Jews Who Love Their History, Heritage, and Community.* New York: Citadel, 2001.

Silver, Mitchell. *Respecting the Wicked Child: A Philosophy of Secular Jewish Identity and Education.* Amherst, MA: University of Massachusetts Press, 1998.

Spinoza, Baruch. *Complete Works: Spinoza.* Michael Morgan, ed. Translated by Samuel Shirley. Indianapolis, IN: Hackett, 2002.

Silverman, Robert. *Baruch Spinoza: Outcast Jew, Universalist Sage.* Northwood, Middlesex, UK: Symposium, 1995.

Smith, Steven. *Spinoza, Liberalism, and the Question of Jewish Identity*. New Haven, CT: Yale University Press, 1997.

Weinberg, David. *Between Tradition and Modernity: Haim Zhitlowski, Simon Dubnow, Ahad Ha-Am, and the Shaping of Jewish Identity*. New York: Holmes and Meier, 1996.

Wine, Sherwin. *Humanistic Judaism*. Buffalo, NY: Prometheus, 1978.

_____. *Celebration: A Ceremonial and Philosophic Guide for Humanists and Humanistic Jews*. Buffalo, NY: Prometheus, 1988.

_____. *The Humanist Haggadah*. Farmington Hills, MI: Society for Humanistic Judaism, 1994.

_____. *Judaism Beyond God*, Hoboken, NJ: KTAV and Milan Press, 1995. Farmington Hills, MI: Society for Humanistic Judaism & Milan Press, 1985, 2010.

_____. *Staying Sane in a Crazy World: A Guide to Rational Living*. Birmingham, MI: Center for New Thinking, 1995. (Available in English and Spanish.)

Yehoshua, A. B. *Diaspora: Exile and the Contemporary Jewish Condition*. Shapolsky, NY: Steimatzky, 1986.

_____. *Mr. Mani*. Translated by Hillel Halkin. San Diego: Harcourt Brace, 1993.

Yerushalmi, Yosef Hayim. *Freud's Moses: Judaism Terminable and Interminable*. New Haven, CT: Yale University Press, 1991.

Yovel, Yirmiyahu. *Spinoza and Other Heretics*. Princeton, NJ: Princeton University Press, 1989.

ANTHOLOGIES
The Posen Library of Jewish Culture and Civilization. New Haven, CT: Yale University Press, 2011.

EDUCATIONAL MATERIALS
Guide to Humanistic Judaism. Farmington Hills, MI: Society for Humanistic Judaism, 1993.

Chalom, Adam. *Introduction to Secular Humanistic Judaism: An Adult Education Curriculum.* IISHJ, 2002/2007/2008.

Gales and Martz, eds. *Apples and Honey: Music and Readings for a Secular Observance of the Jewish New Year Festival.* CSJO, 1995.

Schweitzer, Peter. *The Liberated Haggadah: A Passover Celebration for Cultural, Secular, and Humanistic Jews.* Center for Cultural Judaism, 2003.

Manufactured By: RR Donnelley
Momence, IL USA
December, 2010